What Do Women Really Want?

Edited by Ellen Graham

DOW JONES BOOKS
CHICOPEE, MASS.

Introduction

What do women want anyway?

As the 1960s drew to a close, many people—both men and women—were wondering just that. For seemingly out of nowhere, a social revolution had erupted in the kitchens and offices of this country.

At first, few thought of women's liberation as a revolution. To most—especially men—it was an amusing or, sometimes, infuriating fad perpetuated by a handful of angry feminists that had captured the media's fascination.

These feminists lost no time in announcing what they didn't want: condescension, "protection," boring jobs with no future and low pay, catcalls from construction workers on the street, societal pressure to marry or be ostracized. In short, feminists said they didn't want to be treated like little girls. They proudly proclaimed their womanhood.

Womanhood meant being taken seriously—by their spouses and by their employers. Instead of being a Mrs., many kept their own names, waited longer to marry (if they chose to marry at all) and went to work for its own sake, not just to tide them over until they decided to raise a family and live happily ever after. Most importantly, women declared their right to expanded options; they sought freedom from sexual stereotypes that had customarily channeled them into homemaking rather than, say, homebuilding.

Of course, the call for an upheaval in the delicately balanced sexual power structure that had existed for generations wasn't popular with everyone. Indeed, the movement's validity and significance is still being hotly debated in many quarters of our society. But as it gathered momentum with the help of important equal-rights legislation, more and more ordinary women began to recognize that they shared a common sense of anger and inspiration. Increasingly, these women — with their husbands, bosses, parents, children and friends — are wrestling with the changing values and conflicting priorities and possibilities stemming from liberation.

This is a book about these changes and conflicts. It begins with two portraits — both anachronisms. The first concerns a group for whom women's liberation is nothing new: the suffragettes. For members of the National Women's Party, getting the vote was only the beginning. They've been working for equal rights ever since. The second portrait examines the workaday world of Miss America as she stumps the country plugging Oldsmobiles and Frigidaires. During the 1960s, many women rejected the demurely passive, cosmeticized ideal of womanhood that Miss America represents, an ideal they had long been urged to emulate.

The remainder of the book is concerned with changes in three wide areas: work, the family and education.

You will read how new federal laws and a flurry of important lawsuits have made the topic of hiring and advancing women a top-priority item on most corporate agendas. But what about the women who have taken on jobs formerly reserved exclusively for men? They are turning up on every rung of the corporate ladder, from assembly line to executive suite. You'll learn about their plans and problems, and what they think about their jobs and their male associates. You'll read, too, about complaints from men that they are now the victims of reverse discrimination.

You'll also read how the new pressure on business to attract and keep female employes is forcing modifications in traditional corporate policies of part-time work and maternity leave. You'll learn how equal rights works both ways; how "men's liberationists" are turning sex-discrimination laws to their advantage. And businessmen will find here a short course in how to sidestep embarrassing blunders in their everyday dealings with businesswomen.

Inevitably, the parade of women into the labor force has left its mark on the home. In one chapter, you'll read how men are sharing housework and childrearing to allow their wives to pursue careers. Another story tells how housewives are excluded from social security and disability benefits. You'll read about efforts to end such discrimination that have arisen from the recognition that housework has an intrinsic, quantifiable economic value of its own. In another chapter, you'll meet Anne Adams, housewife, who has moved around the country seven times in nine years following her husband's ascending career. She has a lot to say about the price housewives often pay for their husband's success—in loneliness and plain hard work.

And what of marriage and the family? One article explores the movement to overhaul the nation's antiquated divorce laws. Another describes a young woman's wrenching, yet productive, adjustment to divorced life. In another chapter, you'll discover the social and economic reasons behind the recent steep decline in the birth rate.

Finally, you'll read about a new type of campus revolt, in which women educators are demanding pay and advancement equal to that of their male counterparts. You'll find out about women's studies, or consciousness-raising for credit, and the growing influx of older women who are returning to campus to get degrees. On the elementary and high school level, you'll learn about efforts to end sexism in textbooks and curriculum and squelch the subliminal message that "boys, not blondes, have more fun."

We hope these articles, all of which originally appeared in The Wall Street Journal, will serve as a useful guide to some of the issues raised by the women's movement. These issues go beyond women's rights. The message is human liberation—from a kind of tyranny based on rigid sexual role distinctions. Whatever your feelings about that goal, these articles suggest the feminist movement is likely to have a lasting impact on your life.

—ELLEN GRAHAM
Editor

Contents

Contents

THE NEW AMERICAN FAMILY

Contents

CAMPUS REVOLT

What Do Women Really Want?

Still Kicking

SLIGHTLY faded now, the yellow banner hangs over the stairway inside the big old house on Washington, D.C.'s Capitol Hill. In bold red letters it proclaims: "We demand an amendment to the United States Constitution enfranchising women."

The banner is a memento of a battle won Aug. 26, 1920—the day U.S. women got the right to vote. But the victorious suffragettes didn't stop there. Today, they're still organized (their headquarters is the historic old house), still militant—and close to winning another major victory.

The current goal of the National Woman's Party, founded in 1913 to push for the suffrage amendment, is another amendment. This one would provide that "equality of rights under the law shall not be denied or abridged by the United States or any state on account of sex." With awesome singlemindedness, the party has been fighting for this amendment since 1920.

[The Equal Rights Amendment, repeatedly—and unsuccessfully—introduced in Congress since 1923, was passed by the House in 1971 and the Senate in 1972. If ratified by three-fourths of the states, the amendment would wipe out all distinctions as to sex in state and federal laws.]

A visitor to the vine-covered headquarters, whose front hall is lined with busts and portraits of such de-

3

termined-looking women as Susan B. Anthony and a life-sized statue of Joan of Arc, is promptly asked: "Are you for what we're trying to do?" The next question: "Who's your Congressman?"

Asking those questions is Alice Paul, white-haired and 85 years old, the indomitable founder and honorary chairman of the party. Miss Paul has spent a lifetime crusading for equal legal rights for women, and she brooks no nonsense in discussing that goal. "I can't shout, 'I want my Constitutional rights,' because I don't have any," she says in a typical overstatement.

Title VII of the 1964 Civil Rights Act included provisions forbidding discrimination in employment for reason of sex. Miss Paul says the provision is fine as far as it goes, but her party would prefer protection included in the Constitution itself, rather than a law that might be repealed or altered sometime in the future. In addition, the amendment would go far beyond the area of employment—affecting laws of all kinds that make distinctions as to sex.

Back in the '20s, amid the afterglow of its successful enfranchisement fight, the party was ready to disband, until some wage-earning women convinced its leaders that women needed more than the right to vote. The women showed up at what had been intended as the party's final meeting and told members how they had just lost their jobs because of new labor laws governing women. "They said they were glad to have the right to vote," says Miss Paul. "But that didn't enable them to pay their rent or get an education for their children." Party leaders agreed—committing themselves to a fight tougher than they ever imagined.

"We said yes without realizing what we were getting into," says Miss Paul. "This amendment turned out to be harder than suffrage. Suffrage didn't take anything away from men. But now men feel that women's equal rights will mean competition for them—so they've invented laws that they say are to protect women."

In Miss Paul's view such laws (regulations restricting evening work for women, for example) actually are subtly discriminatory, because their effect is to bar women from certain jobs. The whole thrust of the party's decades-long campaign has been to get this idea across to the public. Initially, women were as hard to convince—or interest—as men.

In 1924, when Congress first held hearings on the amendment, 16 women's organizations showed up to speak against it, Miss Paul relates. The National Woman's Party was the sole supporter. Throughout the struggle, says Miss Paul, "it's strange that so few women (have) cared very much about freedom or the status of women."

But a lot has happened since 1924: The women's liberation movement, for example. It might seem that this burgeoning movement would please Miss Paul. But, "I don't even know what women's lib wants," she says.

Another party officer, Mary Glenn Newell, has some idea, however. "All these liberation women are asking for things that don't come under the amendment. They're for legalizing abortion and dividing the wealth," she says. "The equal rights amendment is not going to help them do that—at least I hope it won't."

"We're not working to have women throw their bras away," she declares, adding: "Why do they want to throw their bras away?"

Miss Paul believes that if women get the equal rights amendment, much could follow. "After we get equal rights and some little power, it is up to women to get these other things like child care," she explains. She's a bit miffed by the suggestions of some other women's groups that they'd make common cause if only the goals of the National Woman's Party were more far-reaching.

"When we were going to prison for the vote, people were saying, 'If only you were going for these other things—like full equal rights—then we would go with you,' " she says. "Now they say, 'if only you were interested in redistributing the wealth. . . .' "

Party members have won over most women's organizations by making the rounds of every such organization in the country, attending conventions and asking support. The chief remaining opposition now is organized labor, although the United Auto Workers and the Teamsters now support the amendment.

Miss Paul says she is a member of The National Organization for Women (NOW), probably the most legislatively oriented of all the feminist groups. NOW joined the Woman's Party as a leading battler for the equal rights amendment in Congress, and its legislative vice president, Brenda Fasteau, has high praise for the erstwhile suffragettes.

The National Woman's Party, she says, has been "really fighting for equal rights ever since the 19th amendment, and they've been pretty singleminded about it." Although Miss Fasteau has occasionally disagreed with the party on tactics, she declares: "Their spirit is exactly in the right place."

A leading supporter of the amendment, Rep. Martha Griffiths (D., Mich.), agrees. "They're the real promoters (of the amendment) without any question," she says. In the years since the amendment was first introduced, "the Woman's Party never forgot."

1970   —CAROL H. FALK

Mi$$ America

THERE she is, Miss America, demure and smiling at a cranberry juice-and-ginger ale reception. And there he is, Harold Wells, hovering at her side. When Miss America smiles for pictures, Mr. Wells beams.

Mr. Wells is the local Oldsmobile dealer in Whiteville, N.C., and on this day Miss America is here promoting Oldsmobiles for him. She spends part of her day taping commercials for Wells Olds, takes some time to sign autographs for his customers and graces the Wells Olds booth at the Columbus County Merchants and Farmers Exposition, where she hands out autographed photos of herself.

Her day, which begins at five in the morning when a chaperone awakens her in the bridal suite at the Carriage Inn in Huntsville, Ala., doesn't end till 10 p.m., when she signs her name to the last of 30 wooden plaques being used as promotions by Mr. Wells. During the day, she signs her name hundreds of times. She has neither the time nor the inclination to watch TV (except to glimpse herself on local newscasts), read or do anything but fall asleep at the end of her long day, for she must be up at seven a.m. the next day to leave for another town.

Whiteville (pop.: 4,683) isn't more than 450 miles from Atlantic City, but, for Miss America at least, the two places are worlds apart. Atlantic City is tears and flowers, Bert Parks and television and misty visions of being Queen for a Year. But Atlantic City lasts just for one night in September, and then it's Whiteville and points South and Midwest. Before she knows it, that's a Harold Wells, not Bert Parks, at her side, and the tears are from hard work and long hours, not happiness. For it's in the nation's Whitevilles where Miss America pays for her title by plugging Oldsmobiles and Frigidaires and Toni beauty products.

Like her less famous colleagues, Miss Wool or Miss Blueberry, Miss America devotes most of her year-long reign to commercial appearances, concentrating on the small-to-medium-sized towns where people still think of Miss America as the pure and fresh-scrubbed symbol of American girlhood. To these people, says an Oldsmobile official, Miss America, stylish but prim, "is something that represents what America should be—like going to a ball game, eating hotdogs or getting kissed on your 16th birthday."

This view of the ideal young girl isn't widely held in big cities today, however, which prompted Pepsi-Cola to drop its cosponsorship of the pageant and the tour in 1968. Pepsi sells best in big cities, and, a company spokesman says, the company decided that the "Miss America pageant as run today does not represent the changing values of our society." In other words, Miss America, a girl with chaperones and without miniskirts, doesn't swing with the Pepsi Generation. Some local Pepsi bottlers still sponsor Miss America's appearances, however.

But other marketing experts point out that 80 million Americans watched the Miss America pageant on television in the fall of 1969—more than watched the final game of the World Series that year—and these people, the experts say, are inclined to buy what Miss America seeks to sell. "Miss America helps us sell to the cross-section of America," says the Oldsmobile man. A woman from the Toni division of Gillette adds, "She appeals to the type of woman who doesn't go to Kenneth to have her hair done."

And so Miss America spends most of the year after her coronation as a pretty and protected salesman. "The sooner you realize you're a product, the better," says Maria Fletcher Growden, Miss America of 1962.

Miss America of 1970—her name is Pamela Anne Eldred, but that name means little to her audiences—is inclined to look upon her role as something more noble than selling cars and refrigerators and shampoo, however. She views herself as sort of a goodwill ambassador whose message is that the girl next door *can* become Miss America. (But so far, no black girl next door has ever made it to the pageant in Atlantic City.)

"I am representing the average middle-class person," says the 21-year-old blonde, measuring her words carefully as she always seems to. "I am representing the typical girl, not someone who's outstanding at all. I enjoy the people I'm meeting. I feel I'm getting an education by doing this."

She is also getting a $10,000 scholarship and an estimated $80,000 in cash. The scholarship comes from the Olds, Frigidaire and Toni people, who sponsor the TV pageant and who can hire her for local appearances at bargain rates. The $80,000 comes from these local appearances—$250 (plus expenses) for an appearance for an Olds, Frigidaire or Toni merchant, $500 for a charitable event and $1,000 for other appearances.

To earn this, Miss America works hard and travels far. Before Miss Eldred's reign is over she will have traveled about 200,000 miles, officials of the Miss America pageant estimate. What's her life like? Cloistered and rugged. In a recent week, more or less typical, she smiled through five cities, 10 formal appearances, three

press conferences and two parades. But she had no
dates, saw no movies and was seldom out of sight of her
chaperone, who is the mother of a former Miss America.

Her week began in Elizabeth City, N.C., a city of
17,000 where the local Pepsi bottler and the Junior
Chamber of Commerce sponsored her visit. There, she
pushed Pepsi and presided at the Miss Elizabeth City
contest, one of about 3,500 contests across the nation
where 70,000 girls enter with the hopes of advancing to
Atlantic City. Besides Miss America, the local pageant
featured the current Miss North Carolina.

"When the boys in Williamston (a nearby town)
found out I had a Miss America and a Miss North Carolina, too, they'd like to die," says Walter Bulliner, the
chairman of the Elizabeth City pageant. Businessmen
might have been impressed, but local beauties weren't.
Only seven girls showed up to compete for Miss Elizabeth City, and Mr. Bulliner concedes that "we had to
beg them to be in it." Originally, 10 girls were persuaded
to enter, but two backed out and a third got so nervous
she broke out in hives.

According to one Jaycee member, the presence of
Miss America was considered the biggest cultural event
in Elizabeth City since a team of Danish gymnasts came
to town in 1968. Indeed, stores closed when the Perqui-
mas County Marching Band led the Miss Elizabeth City
pageant parade down Church Street.

Waving from a red Oldsmobile convertible (Miss
America rides only in Oldsmobiles), Miss America was
clearly living up to what she is supposed to be. "She's
the girl every father wants for a daughter and every boy
wants for a girl friend," as Jacquelyn Meyer Townsend,
Miss America of 1963, sees it.

Some 900 people showed up at the elementary
school auditorium to see Miss America and to watch the
festivities. J. Holland Webster, mayor and owner of two

local movie houses, was on hand. (But Mrs. Webster was not. She was selling movie tickets at one of his theaters.) Miss America, who is majoring in speech and drama at college, gave a speech.

"Can you look in the mirror the next day and say you did your best?" said the girl who entered the Miss Michigan pageant twice before winning and going on to become Miss America. "If you can, then you're a winner in your own heart." Miss North Carolina sang "Summertime" and then the seven contestants paraded in evening gowns and swimming suits. The winner was then crowned amid tears and flashbulbs.

Early the next day, Miss America departed for a quick visit to Washington, D.C. and then on to Huntsville, Ala., for a benefit for a private school. In Washington, Miss Eldred visited a veterans hospital, where she signed autographs. (She received no fee for this visit.) Here she showed a bent for diplomacy. "Where's your home?" the girl from Birmingham, Mich., would invariably ask the patients. "Chicago—the bad side," replied one man. "I didn't know Chicago had a bad side," the beauty replied, moving gracefully on to the next patient.

In Washington, too, Miss America discussed politics. She likes to speak out on national issues, she says, "in order to show people that we're not just brainless Barbie dolls." She doesn't believe in the protests against the war and against the President, she said in Washington, and she added: "I think we forget that the President isn't the only person that has anything to do with us being in the war. There's a Congress. And they too have to agree with him or else we wouldn't be over there. At least, that's what I learned in school."

In the past, some Miss Americas have had to be coached on what to say and what not to say, but nobody has to coach Miss Eldred because her main goal is to "be a credit to the Miss America pageant." She not only tries to avoid inflammatory statements but also doesn't smoke, drink or swear. All this makes easy work for her two chaperones, who alternate months with her.

The chaperones' main duties are to brief "Miss A" (as she is known to pageant officials) on the planned activities, ensure that she rides only in Oldsmobiles and enforce the pageant rule prohibiting men from kissing Miss America. (The rule apparently doesn't apply to dates, though the chaperone is supposed to go along on any dates so no boy is likely to get too fresh. Miss Eldred, who was not going with any particular boy before she was crowned, didn't go out on a date for months after she won the title.)

The chaperones are ever protective. Once, while staying in a girls' dormitory at the University of Texas, Miss Eldred was awakened by a light in her bedroom. "Don't be afraid, Pam," said Mrs. Irene Bryant, her chaperone, as she shined a flashlight under Miss America's bed. "A man has sneaked into the dorm." Another night, when Miss Eldred complained her room was too cold, she crawled into bed with Mrs. Bryant to keep warm.

Because of her tight schedule, Miss America has little free time to read, think, loaf, or, if she wanted to, date. She spends most of what extra time she has writing thank-you notes to well-wishers, setting her hair and seeing that her clothes are cleaned and pressed and packed. She travels lightly for a clotheshorse, carrying her six dresses and gowns in two pink suitcases. She also packs a couple of tote bags. Much of her wardrobe is replaced every month or so when she gets home or back to headquarters in Atlantic City.

Miss America wore a purple suit, with hem three inches above the knees, for her flight from Washington to Huntsville, a city of 125,000 in northern Alabama.

She changed outfits several times in Huntsville, because, among other things, she had to appear in three fashion shows. At each show, she gave a speech: "If the people of Alabama are as warm as the people in Huntsville, then all I can say is that I hope I can return to Alabama." By the third show, her ending had changed to, "I hope I can make Alabama my home."

Miss Eldred never lost her poise, even when some youths accidentally spilled Pepsi on the fashion show runway. She willingly posed with everyone from the police who were escorting her to wide-eyed sales girls. She smiled whenever the occasion called for it. Huntsville citizens were clearly delighted. "The last Miss America who came here was a pill," confided a local leader. "She never smiled unless she was in front of a camera."

Miss Eldred, who learned her perfect posture in night school courses at Patricia Stevens Finishing School in Detroit, concedes that sometimes there are many things she would rather do than smile. "Many days I'm tired and really don't want to go on and smile," she says. "But I feel I am Miss America and I have accepted an obligation to do this—just as someone accepts an obligation to sell cars."

Miss Eldred's smiling and striving to please elate the sponsors of the Miss America pageant. "She does a great face-to-face job," says the man at Oldsmobile. "She's the kind of girl who will thank everyone from the janitor on up for her being Miss America."

Sponsors and pageant officials have not been happy with every Miss America. Mrs. Townsend, the 1963 winner, remembers that she had exceptionally long hair during her reign—at a time when Toni was sponsoring the short-hair look. "We used to just grit our teeth and wish she'd cut it," says a Toni official.

Miss Eldred was smiling prettily and pleasing folks again early the next morning when she arrived in

Whiteville from Huntsville for her appearances on behalf of Wells Olds and the Merchants and Farmers Exposition. At the exposition, she competed with exhibits featuring live sheep, a moonshine still and motorboats, but she was by far the biggest attraction.

It was a Thursday that Miss America spent in Whiteville, and early Friday morning she took off for Detroit, where she spent the weekend appearing for Oldsmobile at the big Detroit Auto Show. The auto show was old hat to her—she had worked there as a model for American Motors in past years — but it gave her a chance to be close to her family in Birmingham.

But the moments with her family were few. On Monday morning, she was up early and off to Poteau, Okla. The local Oldsmobile dealer had a big day planned for her.

1970   —MARY BRALOVE

Working Women

Corporate Liberation

IF the women's liberation movement was once treated as a major joke in the boardrooms of corporate America—as most women say it was—the laughter now is ringing hollow. Companies across the country now are finding that they're going to have to come to grips quickly with demands for women's equality on pain of substantial financial penalties.

"This thing is going so fast that some companies are being dragged kicking and screaming into 1972," says John Naisbitt, president of Urban Research Corp., a Chicago-based social research outfit. The issue of women's rights Mr. Naisbitt adds, "is going to be to the '70s what (the issue of) civil rights was to the '60s."

The major impetus behind this acceleration is the federal government. Until recently, the government drive against sex bias has been concentrated in the nation's universities—attempting, with varying degrees of success, to force the academic institutions to eliminate sex discrimination in hiring. Now, however, the government has responded to increasing pressure from women's groups and has turned its spotlight on America's corporations.

The federal spotlight will be focused primarily on corporate compliance to an order ("Revised Order 4") issued in December 1971 by the Secretary of Labor. The highly complex directive requires prime government contractors and subcontractors with 50 or more employes and government contracts of $50,000 or more to set specific goals and timetables for moving qualified women into all levels of their work forces—and if the companies don't comply, the government will revoke federal contracts.

The implications of the government's attention haven't been lost on many companies. "If management can read the tea leaves, they're going to have to develop pro-active stances towards women," says Jan Blakslee, head of minority hiring at Cummins Engine Co. in Columbus, Ind. "For one thing, it's going to cost them a bundle if they don't."

While the message from Washington has been loud and clear, many corporations are finding that the implementation of sex-equality directives is a step into a little-known area. "We're all on a starting basis," says Carol Clapp, an officer in Boise Cascade Corp.'s equal-opportunity department. "There has been a complete circle in a year—to where companies now are saying, 'Maybe this is a common problem we all have, and maybe we can actually look at this and help each other.' "

From a woman's standpoint, certainly, the problem is acute. According to Department of Labor statistics, the median wage in 1970 of women (who constituted slightly more than one-third of the civilian work force) was 59.4% of the median wage of men—a *decrease* from nearly 64% in 1955. What's more, when broken down by occupations and educational levels, the income of women was consistently below that of men in the same categories.

A highly visible—and highly controversial—area of sex discrimination has been the world of white-collar workers. The Labor Department reports that in 1971 women accounted for 38% of all workers but filled only

17% of all managerial posts. Furthermore, a survey by two professors at Stanford University and the University of Michigan of 300 of the nation's 500 largest industrial corporations disclosed that the companies were employing women executives at only one-fifth the national rate—and most of these women executives, the survey said, were clustered in a few women's-products firms.

But the women want more than equal opportunity and equal pay for equal work. They are demanding, and in at least one instance are getting, such other benefits as company-sponsored day-care centers for their children, increased time and sick pay for maternity leaves, and revised hiring procedures that will disregard a woman's marital status and other information considered by many women to be discriminatory.

Women have been making attempts for decades to improve their status in corporate America, but their large-scale, concentrated assault on male business bastions dates back only to the early 1960s. The 1963 passage of the Equal Pay Act (an amendment to the Fair Labor Standards Act of 1938) and the Civil Rights Act of 1964 fueled the feminist movement, and the pace of the assault was further quickened in 1971, when the Labor Department issued its Revised Order 4.

Some skeptics, doubting ultimate beneficial results, point to the fact that the order leans heavily on the "good faith" of the companies involved. While the companies' compliance is subject to government inspection, cynics say those firms that don't comply won't be taken to task very quickly; prior to contract revocation, offenders will be warned and then allowed a hearing to present their side. And according to the order, "every effort" will be made to settle matters through "conciliation, mediation and persuasion."

Nevertheless, some women are pleased. For example, Aileen Hernandez, head of the national advisory board of the National Organization for Women, calls Revised Order 4 "one of our signal victories."

Despite this elation, no one—least of all the women involved—believes that Revised Order 4 is going to eliminate sex discrimination overnight. The major thrust of the order, for example, is concerned with long-range planning. And since short-term benefits can't be expected to any great degree, many companies can expect to face an increasing number of irate women employes in court.

Many of these court challenges will probably be based on the government's Equal Pay Act, enacted in 1963. (The act essentially requires that men and women receive equal pay for equal work. Under the act, the Labor Department or individuals can file court suits to seek redress for alleged pay discrimination.)

One large settlement under the Equal Pay Act involved Wheaton Glass Co. in Millville, N.J., which has paid more than $901,000 in back salaries and interest to women employes. The case was brought to court by the Labor Department when the women claimed they'd been paid less than men for similar work. In another settlement, the Labor Department in 1972 won a judgment in U.S. District Court against Pacific Telephone & Telegraph Co. The company has since paid $450,000 in back pay and interest to women employes found eligible under the Equal Pay Act.

In most sex-discrimination cases, the courts have assessed companies for back pay plus 6% interest. While most of these cases have been initiated by the Labor Department, the Department of Justice is also active in sex-bias matters. Under Title VII of the Civil Rights Act, for example, the Justice Department obtained a consent order under which Household Finance Corp. agreed to pay more than $125,000 in back pay to about 175 women employes who had alleged that they had been denied promotions because of their sex. (Household Finance, however, denied the government's allegations of discrimination.)

The Equal Employment Opportunity Commission has also been heavily involved in the area of women's corporate rights. In the government's fiscal year, ended June 30, 1971, complaints of discrimination by women accounted for nearly 25% of the total charges filed by the commission. [In 1973, American Telephone & Telegraph Co. agreed in a federal administrative proceeding to pay about $15 million in restitution and equal pay to 13,000 women and 2,000 male minority members. In addition, 36,000 workers will receive $23 million a year in higher pay. During the proceeding, the EEOC called the Bell System "without doubt the largest oppressor of women workers in the United States." AT&T denied the charges.]

The growing number of complaints, allegations, petitions and reports concerning sex discrimination is creating more than passing concern in big business. "I don't think that companies any more are feeling that all this will blow over," says Robert A. Madison, minority-affairs consultant for Sun Oil Co. Sun, like many other concerns, is currently studying its work force to locate women employes qualified for promotion to higher positions. The company has also given its college recruiters quotas to fill on the hiring of newly graduated women. (Sun declines, however, to give details concerning such quotas.)

While most big companies are grappling with the problem of getting more women into all levels of their work forces, some are also dealing with the more nebulous problem of changing long-held corporate attitudes toward women. For example, General Electric Co. and Boise Cascade have instituted "management awareness" sessions for their employes, during which the problem of sex discrimination is discussed.

Going beyond discussions, International Business Machines Corp., which requires all its managers to participate in a three-hour program on sex bias, commissioned a $50,000 film, for managerial viewing, on problems that confront workers. The film, about a half-hour long, explores sex-discrimination in the lives of three businesswomen: a young secretary, whose husband warns her that women don't have a chance in the business world; a middle-level worker with impressive academic and professional experience who realizes that she's in a rut; and a woman in management who confronts the problem of working with the man who had unsuccessfully vied for her job.

Despite the flurry of activity, almost all companies concede that they have thus far made little progress toward the elimination of sex discrimination. "You'll find some movement, but I think it will be slow," says a personnel expert with one industrial concern. "I think you'll find tokenism to be rampant. It's going to take a lot of time and lot of court cases."

Some companies, however, report encouraging signs. At IBM, for example, the number of women managers increased 9% in 1971 from 1970. Additionally, IBM says that more than 20% of its women employes received promotions last year. Less specifically, the company says its men's-promotion figure for 1971 was "in the same ball park" as that of its women.

The elimination of sex bias, of course, must go further than ending rank and salary discrimination. Boise Cascade rewrote its employment application form to delete all questions about dependents, marital status, and the name and employment of the applicant's spouse. AT&T has established two experimental child-care centers in Washington, D.C., and Columbus, Ohio, for children of both male and female employes; the company picks up half of the $6-a-day cost for each child. Control Data Corp. has invited other companies to share the facilities of an inner-city day-care center that it recently set up in the vicinity of one of its plants. And a number of concerns allow women on maternity leave to collect six weeks sick pay.

The exact federal requirements concerning the elimination of sex discrimination have confused more than one company. "I haven't found many companies that are unwilling to get into working against sex discrimination if they'd just be told what to do and know the rules won't be changed when they're halfway through the program," says David W. Pearson, president of National Compliance Co., a Dallas firm that consults companies on federal contract compliance.

Some observers, however, argue that many companies, by simply worrying about regulatory compliance, are missing the wider implications of women's drive for equality. "Too many executives see this as a compliance problem, instead of seeing it as an opportunity to draw from this extraordinarily talented labor pool in ways that for the first time are socially acceptable, even if not corporately acceptable," says Urban Research Corp.'s Mr. Naisbitt.

But with or without regulations and government orders, many women's-rights proponents are optimistic about the future of their movement. "If there weren't laws on the books and weren't people in the courts, there would still be the women's movement rolling along," asserts Aileen Hernandez of the National Organization for Women. "You might as well face it— women aren't going to go away."

1972 —ERIC MORGENTHALER

Flexing a Muscle

TODAY'S public-service announcement from the Labor Department:

Announcer: "High noon in Gotham City. . . . In a deserted warehouse Batman and Robin are shackled to a post—desperately struggling to break loose! Inches away, a time bomb ticks ominously . . . suddenly, a crash of glass!"

Robin: "Holy breaking and entering! It's Batgirl!"

Batman: "Quick, Batgirl, untie us before it's too late!"

Batgirl: "It's already too late. I've worked for you a long time, and I'm paid less than Robin."

Robin: "Holy discontent!"

Batgirl: "Same employer, same job means equal pay for men and women."

Batman: "This is no time for jokes, Batgirl."

Batgirl: "It's no joke—it's the Federal Equal Pay Law."

The radio message is corny, but it's risky for employers to scoff. Because for thousands of women, the principle of equal pay for equal work is taking on real dollar-and-cents meaning as a result of federal lawsuits, private litigation and just plain protests from the female ranks.

For example:

—Andrea Logan received $1,750 in back pay from

the Chesapeake & Potomac Telephone Co. in Washington as part of a massive $7.5 million equal-pay settlement involving several federal agencies and the Bell System. Mrs. Logan, who works as a "frameman" connecting telephone equipment in a central office, says her pay has increased by about $45 a week, to $198. The specific reason: added allowance for seniority. She's getting credit for her entire seven years with the company rather than just her 18 months on the present job.

—Some 350 women at a General Electric Co. plant in Fort Wayne received raises totaling $250,000 a year plus an estimated $300,000 in back pay in the settlement of an equal-pay lawsuit brought by the International Union of Electrical Workers.

—Faculty members at the University of Louisville have negotiated about $60,000 a year in pay raises designed to correct inequities for 41 women. Inez Webb, a professor of home economics who has taught at the school since 1946, is getting about $1,000, or nearly 10%, more in annual pay. Such changes, she suggests, "will make a difference" to young women who seek teaching jobs and scrutinize male vs. female pay comparisons.

The government, unions, women's groups and individual women are all increasingly measuring employer practices against the demands of the Equal Pay Act passed by Congress in 1963. That law, in essence, requires the same pay for the same work done by men and women.

Federal enforcers, in particular, are bearing down harder. In the early days of the law, the Labor Department was finding that employers owed back-pay totaling $2 million to $3 million a year. But court decisions broadening the scope of the Equal Pay Act helped boost the sum to $18 million in the fiscal year ended June 30, 1973. As of that date, the department's investigations found that more than 140,000 workers, most of them women, were owed more than $72 million.

This figure will presumably swell further. Dozens of new lawsuits are likely to be filed, by both the government and private plaintiffs, as the result of recent broadening of the law. In 1972, an additional 15 million workers in executive, administrative, educational and outside-sales jobs were brought under its coverage; most hourly paid workers were already protected.

Yet in spite of the years of enforcement effort, there remains considerable resistance to the idea of equal pay for equal work. Francis W. McGowan, director of the Labor Department's division of equal pay and employment standards, says that society still has "this widespread belief that when women work it isn't worth as much as when men work."

Without question, a huge gap still exists between the wages of male and female workers. In 1971, federal figures show, women working full-time earned $5,593, or about 60%, of the $9,399 median earnings of men. Differences of that magnitude have existed since the mid-1950s.

Much of the gap, of course, has nothing to do with deliberate refusal to equalize wages. Men often have more work experience than women of the same age. Men often receive more job training and education. With women excluded from many higher-paying jobs, an oversupply of female applicants for less desirable positions tends to depress their wages. In such cases, "the law of supply and demand is stronger than the Equal Pay Act," Barbara R. Bergmann, a University of Maryland professor, told a congressional hearing in 1973.

After experience and training factors are removed, there remains a wage differential of perhaps 30% that can "be regarded as the result of discriminatory treatment in the labor market," Marina Whitman and Herbert Stein of the President's Council of Economic Advisers told the same hearing. (Mrs. Whitman has since left the council.)

The Equal Pay Act attempts to bridge that gap. And failure to comply can be costly for employers.

First, the law permits recovery of back wages up to two years from the time a suit is filed. Second, interest may be imposed on the unpaid wages; in some cases, the interest alone has approached $250,000. Third, if a private party brings the suit, the worker may seek up to twice the amount of lost wages; "a private lawyer can make a good income from double damages," says one New York attorney. Finally, wages must be raised to the proper level, affecting current and future labor costs.

Particularly for jobs newly covered by the law, there is "a real incentive for employers to dig in and do something," says Barbara Ashley Phillips, a San Francisco lawyer. "They have no choice, and the price is only going to go up."

Until recently, Mr. McGowan of the Labor Department says, many employers haven't given equal pay "the priority they ought to; they may be more concerned about the demurrage on a freight car being unloaded." But the sizable back-pay awards now have caught corporate attention. Philip S. Braun, a wage and salary controls consultant at General Electric Co., says, "There has been a slow realization among employers, but it has come home to them as these court cases are decided."

In 1970, in the first major appellate decision interpreting the law, a federal circuit court of appeals upheld a $900,000 back-pay award to a group of women workers at Wheaton Glass Co. in Millville, N.J. Significantly, the court expanded the law to cover "substantially equal" work done by women, rather than tasks identical to those done by males.

Court decisions and administrative interpretations have confirmed that to remedy the discrimination, lower rates paid one sex must be raised to the higher rates paid the other sex. An employer can't cut male workers' pay to equalize rates, and it can't circumvent the law by replacing an all-male work force with lower-paid women or by certain other subterfuges. In early 1973, a circuit court ruled that a Texas drug company broke the law when it paid a woman who filled a vacant job less than it had paid the man who previously held the post.

Equal-pay decisions have forced a number of hospitals to adjust pay for female nurse's aides to equal rates paid male orderlies. In 1972, an Oil City, Pa., hospital agreed to pay a group of women $25,000 to bring their pay in line with that of men who had received about 30 cents an hour more. "The primary duties of the aides and orderlies are identical," a federal judge found.

A number of school districts and colleges have been forced to raise pay for women janitorial help. In Pennsylvania, a U.S. district judge found 24 women at Grove City College earning $1.35 to $1.55 an hour, while four men on the janitorial staff earned $1.90 to $2.25. Although the men occasionally moved furniture and used hand tools for repairs, the wage differential couldn't be justified, the judge said. He found 95% of the work identical.

Determining discrimination among retail sales workers isn't so simple, however. In early 1973, the third circuit court found Robert Hall Clothes Inc. could pay salesmen more than saleswomen—almost $1 an hour more in 1969—because the men's clothing department where the men worked produced greater economic benefits for the company. But the fifth circuit in May 1973 ordered Loveman's Department Store in Montgomery,

Ala., to equalize rates paid salesmen and saleswomen and also those paid tailors and seamstresses; in that case, the court found the work was substantially equal.

The Equal Pay Law's expansion to cover executive, administrative and professional employes also promises new legal skirmishes soon. "The biggest issue in 1974 will probably be in the educational institutions," suggests Carin Ann Clauss, associate solicitor in the Labor Department. "We know that is an area of mass violations." (A U.S. Office of Education survey found male college professors in 1972-73 earned an average $19,128 while female professors earned $16,950; at the instructor level, men earned $10,964, while women earned $10,089.)

1973   —JAMES C. HYATT

Rosie Returns

R OSIE is back.

When American men went off to World War II, their wives and sisters and mothers and grandmothers stepped onto production lines to keep the factories humming. "Rosie the Riveter" became a popular song, and the nation's Rosies became heroines of the war effort. But the war ended, and Rosie quit her job and went back to running a home instead of a drill press.

But women increasingly are returning to blue-collar jobs. Now, however, it isn't to support any war effort. Nor is it to flex their rights and strike blows for women's liberation. Rather, it's for a more basic reason: money.

"Most of my friends are secretaries making about $300 a month," says 20-year-old Stella Barens. "That's peanuts to me." Miss Barens works for Davidson Volkswagen in Lorain, Ohio, diagnosing auto ills and poking around greasy VW engines. She earns $700 a month.

In Cleveland, Edith Newsome became a production-line worker two years ago for Republic Steel Co. She helps process big steel slabs at the end of the line, and she earns $4.11 an hour. That's considerably better than the $2.85 an hour she made as a sweeper in the company's cold-rolled sheet department. And it's more than most clerks and secretaries at Republic earn.

Mary Hilton, deputy director of the women's bureau of the U.S. Department of Labor, predicts a "dramatic" rise in such employment in the next three to five years. There are several reasons. More employers are living up to the spirit of the Civil Rights Act of 1964, which requires that men and women be given equal consideration, and to the Equal Pay Act of 1963, which requires equal pay for equal work. Also many employers have been pinched for skilled labor and are discovering that women can do the jobs as well—and at times better —than men.

Moreover, women have been entering the labor market in rising numbers, placing more pressure on the bastions of male jobs. (At the same time, men have been attacking women's strongholds, becoming airplane stewards, telephone operators, secretaries and the like.) Figures aren't available on how many women hold these jobs, but the Census Bureau does report that the percentage of women who work was 42% in 1970, up from 37% in 1960 and 33% in 1950. Women accounted for nearly two-thirds of the increase in the labor force in the past decade.

The higher-paying blue-collar jobs are particularly attractive to women who support themselves and their families. Mary Warren, a 26-year-old widow and mother of two children says, "If I had to work, I figured I'd better make money at it." Mrs. Warren operates a printing press at S. H. Davis Paper Box Co. in Toledo, Ohio, and she is the first female to do so at the company.

Mrs. Warren admits that there was a period of adjustment and that her male counterparts were somewhat stand-offish and skeptical at first. "But when they saw how determined I was and that I wouldn't take any guff, then they learned to accept me," she says.

Mrs. Newsome, the Cleveland steelworker and a 40-year-old divorcee with two children, also had to adjust to her job, but in another way. "Everything moved so fast that at first I didn't think I would be able to handle it," she recalls. "But once I tried it, I found I do better than some men who have been here 20 years." Her superiors agree she is at least as good as some veteran men workers.

The women are getting some help from the courts and the government. In one precedent-setting case, American Telephone & Telegraph Co. recently agreed in a federal administrative proceeding to pay about $15 million in restitution and equal pay claims to 13,000 women and 2,000 male minority-group members. More importantly, the agreement provides that women and minority-group members promoted to new jobs will get credit for company seniority for the time spent on their former jobs as well as time in the higher-paying classifications.

The old policy at American Telephone, allegedly, discouraged women from seeking better jobs because they knew they'd become the first to be eligible for lay-off, having lost their seniority from lower-level jobs.

For some women, the jobs can be a matter of accident. For instance, Interstate Van Lines had a male van driver who "was a good worker, but we could never find him," says Aaron Powell, the company's personnel manager. So, the Springfield, Va., concern hired the man's wife three years ago as "his helper to straighten him out," according to Mr. Powell.

She was the first woman hired by Interstate outside of clerical help, and she proved so adept at packing goods to be moved that the company decided to hire women regularly as packers. Housewives, it seems, prefer female packers who "have a little different feeling toward household items," he says.

At Continental Homes Inc.'s modular-home plant in Nashua, N.H., a woman asked if she could become a carpenter after hearing male workers complain about the difficulty of their work in an effort to get a sizable wage increase. She got the job, handled it well and the company moved several other women into similar jobs.

"They're a lot more dependable," says Raymond Demanche, the plant manager. "They're not speed demons, but we know exactly what we can expect from them."

Sometimes what you can expect isn't what you want. Firestone Tire & Rubber Co. hired two women as tire builders in its Decatur, Ill., plant, but it had to switch them to other jobs. "The problem was they tried to build too good a tire," says an industrial-relations man. "They couldn't keep up with quotas. One of them built a beautiful tire, but she couldn't produce in quantity."

1973   —MICHAEL JETT

Opening the Door

THE motel conference room is plastered with feminist posters, including one of Israeli Premier Golda Meir captioned, "But can she type?" About 40 women, all of them Westinghouse Electric Corp. employes, have gathered in Pittsburgh for a three-day workshop designed to motivate and prepare them for jobs in management. Now, on the final day, the group is debating the extent of sexual discrimination in the business world.

Irene Watson, a personnel representative in her fifties, speaks for the least militant camp: "We don't think women have been denied opportunity," she says. "We disagree with those who feel women should be given special consideration because of their sex. Any woman who wants to succeed, can."

"But a woman shouldn't have to be better than a man to get a job," argues Janet Felmeth, a home economist who speaks for the feminists in the group. "We're not superhuman, and there should be a place for the average woman, just as there is for the average man." She pulls out a book of statistics showing that women college graduates earn on the average more than $5,000 a year less than their male counterparts. "Now won't you agree women have been discriminated against?" she asks.

"Men are making more money because they're

more qualified," retorts Irene. "If you're held back, it isn't because you're a woman, it's because of your own inadequacies."

After hearing both arguments, the other women in the group vote Irene the winner of the debate. Jody Johns, who designed and presented the workshop for Westinghouse Learning Corp., knew that few of the participants would be hard-core feminists. "My objective was to help build confidence," she says. "I wanted to inspire them to aim higher and expect more."

Such confidence-building, inspirational sessions for women are becoming popular in the male dominated world of business. Workshops, seminars, and conferences aimed at preparing women for management are proliferating, as corporations scurry to comply with government pressure to move women into more responsible jobs.

The focal point of this pressure is the Department of Labor's "Revised Order 4," which requires companies with government contracts to set specific goals and timetables for hiring and promoting women on all levels of their work forces. If the companies fail to comply, the government can revoke its contracts.

If Revised Order 4 hasn't exactly thrown the door to the executive suite wide open to women, it has at least pried it open a crack. At Dow Chemical Co., for example, the number of women in professional and managerial jobs jumped 20% between 1972 and 1973. And the number of women managers at IBM Corp. increased 35% in the same period.

The influx of women into management means business is booming for a new breed of consultant specializing in training women executives. The American Management Association, which has sponsored conferences for women managers since 1967, says attendance at these courses "roughly doubled" between 1972 and 1973.

AMR International Inc., a New York-based concern providing advanced training for business executives, reports a "great demand" for its new management-skills seminar for women. And even the Katherine Gibbs School, which for years has specialized in turning Vassar graduates into secretaries, has recently begun offering evening management courses for women.

"Women are hungry for management education," asserts Rosemary LeBoeuf, a program director for the American Management Association. If they are, it's because they have so much catching up to do. Although many critics question the need for specialized programs for women, corporations have traditionally ignored women when selecting promising talent to send to advanced training courses. "Companies with a limited amount of dollars budgeted for such training have typically preferred to send men," says Rosalind Loring, Assistant Dean of UCLA's university extension program, which offers a series of management courses attended by 6,000 women each year.

When a woman does attend a predominantly male training course, the experience can sometimes be unproductive, consultants say. Jody Johns remembers attending a Westinghouse management course where there were 58 male and two female participants. The women, she says, were patronized and intimidated and didn't participate actively. Her observations are borne out in a study by psychiatrist Carol Wolman of the University of Pennsylvania and Hal Frank, assistant professor of management at the University's Wharton School. The researchers found that in groups of men and a lone woman, all of equal professional status, the woman's efforts to participate actively were consistently resisted by the men.

If women have been barred from outside training programs, their on-the-job training has been hit-or-miss, at best. Sexual stereotyping of jobs has often kept women from exposure to skills that would enable them to step into more responsible positions. At the Westinghouse course, for example, most participants complained they hadn't been trained to prepare budgets or write reports.

Most of the new management courses for women provide an overview of modern techniques of decision-making, communication and problem-solving. They also usually give at least a nod to the special psychological problems many women face in making the transition into supervision or management. However, experts disagree about how much emphasis to place on this part of the program. Rosemary LeBoeuf of the American Management Association says, "We stay away from feminist issues. It can easily flake off into a consciousness-raising session." But consciousness-raising was precisely what Jody Johns had in mind: "This isn't a course in management skills," she says. "We're trying to come to grips with the problems we face as women in a man's world."

The 40 or so Westinghouse women who gathered one morning in 1973 to discuss such issues included executive secretaries, first-line supervisors, managers and professionals. Their ages range from the early 20s to the middle 50s. Half are unmarried, and of those who had been married, only nine are still living with their husbands. A poll taken at the opening session turns up only one who claims to be active in the women's movement (although nearly all felt they have been discriminated against at one time or another). All report to men, only three have ever been fired, and half think they are paid fairly. A handful admit nervously that they would rather be somewhere other than the workshop.

Although many of these women are occupying jobs formerly held by men, they display little of the militant feminism often associated with the stereotype of the ambitious career woman. Many express fears of "losing their femininity" as they advance in their work. They admit they find it difficult to deal with resentment from men they supervise or other women who aren't advancing as fast. And they worry about how to resolve the double demands of work and home. "It's more socially acceptable for a man to sacrifice his home for a career than it is for a woman," one says.

Yet, in spite of ambivalence about the price they might be paying for success, few seem willing to give up their aspirations. They discuss ways to break out of dead-end or female-stereotyped jobs, and Jody Johns and Marie Kirn, the group leaders, encourage them to set specific goals for advancement. With the help of other participants, they map strategies to meet their goals.

Introducing an exercise in which participants were asked to list all the functions they perform in their jobs and the skills needed to do so, Marie says, "Women often lack self-confidence. Even if they have the skills, they may still think they are underqualified. Maybe this exercise will show you you're more qualified than you thought." During the discussion, one executive secretary mentions off-handedly that she supervises a group of clerical workers. "But that's a minor aspect of my work," she says. "I'm really not their boss." The group tries to show her that she is soft-pedaling her abilities and that she has more responsibility than she is admitting.

As the workshop progresses, the women seem to gather strength and confidence from sharing similar concerns. "I used to be a male chauvinist pig when it came to other women," says Pat Wells, a systems analyst. "I confided mostly in men. This course has made me like and respect other women more."

Besides discussing issues relating to womanhood and work, the group takes part in simulation exercises aimed at building decision-making skills. In one, they are told that they had survived an airplane crash in the desert and that 15 items that might be helpful to their survival were salvaged from the plane. Each participant is told to rank the items in order of their importance— first individually, and then in a team, which tries to come to a consensus about the ranking order.

When the results are compared with a ranking made by a survival expert, the group decisions prove more accurate than individual decisions. Jody says that results from 2,550 people who had completed the standardized exercise had shown that groups of women scored significantly higher in such decision-making than groups of men or mixed groups.

As the workshop draws to a close, a few participants grumble that it hasn't sufficiently emphasized management techniques. Yet most agree it has had a profound effect on their attitudes about themselves and their jobs.

Pat Proctor, a college recruiter, says, "When I first heard I was being sent to this course, I was furious. I didn't want to sit around with a bunch of women and jaw about how we were discriminated against." But Mrs. Proctor, a divorcee with three teen-aged children, says the course made her rethink her own career objectives. Now she wants a more responsible position. "I want to do something that's measurable," she says, "so I'll be given the credit or blame when it's done." She had previously attended another Westinghouse management course, where she was the only woman participant. "There, I felt I was a token," she says. "I was constantly hiding behind my femininity. Here, I felt more like a real person."

Although courses like the Westinghouse workshop

can do much to motivate and inspire women, some management consultants worry about what happens when the women return to their jobs. The consultants are skeptical about industry's commitment to follow through beyond the training, and they say such courses stir rising expectations that, for the time being at least, the business world is unprepared or unwilling to meet.

"In some cases, companies send women to management-development courses just to quiet them down," says Charles D. Orth, president of Career Development International Inc. of Wellesley, Mass., a consulting firm that provides career guidance for businesswomen.

Most consultants believe that attitudes of men, as well as women, must change before equal opportunity programs can work. UCLA's Rosalind Loring says, "If I had my druthers, I'd plan all my courses for men on how to work with women." And, according to Mr. Orth "If you go into an organization and work only with the women and ignore the men's problems, you threaten the hell out of the men and do your cause damage."

There may be reason for all the concern. After the workshop, Miss Johns abruptly resigned as manager of product development for Westinghouse Learning Corp. She did so, she says, because she was denied a promotion she thinks she deserved. Her division manager had recently resigned and had recommended her for the job. But she wasn't promoted. Instead, the division manager's job was eliminated, and a new management team was set up to make decisions. A man from outside the company was brought in as her boss and assigned to the team.

Westinghouse claims she lacked experience for the division manager's job. "We'd been grooming her for that kind of job, but she isn't at that level yet," says Harvey Brudner, president of Westinghouse Learning Corp. "The man who took the job had a proven track record as a manager." But Jody, who had been with the company six years (three of them as a manager), says, "Men with far less experience than I have had are promoted to general manager regularly." In explaining the reasons for her resignation, she says: "I would have been expected to show my new boss what to do and keep the operation going, while he would have gotten the credit for capable management."

1973   —ELLEN GRAHAM

Where the Boys Are

O N Jan. 18, 1973, the federal Equal Employment Opportunity Commission (EEOC) and American Telephone & Telegraph Co. agreed to settle a job-discrimination suit. The settlement called for the immediate payment of $15 million in restitution and back pay to 15,000 AT&T women and minority employes and the budgeting of $23 million annually for employe wage and promotion benefits.

The corporate world hasn't been the same since.

"Since the AT&T settlement, I get a call once a day from some executive who wants to hire a woman," says an executive recruiter. "Obviously, the heat is on."

The specter of corporate profits disappearing in a cloud of discrimination suits spurred many companies to action. Memos from the top brass came down, and their message was clear—keep the EEOC at bay. Press releases started to roll. Manufacturing companies heralded the promotion of women managers and supervisors. Banks pushed women from tellers' cages to branch managers' offices. Insurance companies encouraged women to enter the actuarial and sales fields. More women then ever before began seeping into middle-management ranks.

Yet what the press releases aren't announcing, what the memos aren't heralding, what the corporations aren't trumpeting is this fact: Few women are progressing beyond the middle level. To be sure, every

once in a while a woman such as Wisconsin banker
Catherine B. Cleary is named to a board of directors.
Every once in a while a woman like Mary Wells gets to
the top of a big enterprise because it's an enterprise
that she built from scratch. Every once in a while a
woman like Katharine Graham becomes a captain of industry because she inherited the job at a family-con-
trolled company.

But by and large, women aren't getting many important corporate posts. Their advancement stops short
of the executive suite, their authority ends short of final
decision-making power. The September-October 1973
issue of the Harvard Business Review reported that out
of 20 major corporations surveyed, employing nearly
two million people, women represent less than 1% of
the officials, managers and professionals.

And in a 1974 issue, the Harvard Business Review
said a survey of 1,500 subscribers revealed that "social
and psychological barriers to women interested in a
management or professional career still exist despite recent changes in policies on the employment of women."

"Women are getting better salaries and titles, but
not the top posts," says Cynthia Epstein, an associate
professor of sociology at Queens College who has studied the progress of businesswomen through the corporate ranks.

This isn't totally because all men are male chauvinist pigs. The apparent chauvinistic attitudes on the part
of businessmen are indeed a major factor—"it's a common pattern that somebody upstairs identifies someone
as 'my fair-haired boy,' " says Prof. Epstein; "they never
think their bright young man could be a bright young
woman." But the outlook on the part of many women is
also a factor—like many men, many women prefer the
enjoyment of family life to longer hours and extra responsibility at work. And so, too, is the fact that many

women lack the education and the experience to get the top jobs in some male-dominated fields such as engineering.

Women still remain a tiny minority even in business schools, for instance. According to the American Assembly of Collegiate Schools of Business, the number of women graduate and doctoral business students has inched up to only 5.5% of such students from 3.1% in 1969.

But if getting to the top is tough, living at the top is even more of a strain for some women. They say they are often belittled, if not insulted, because of the misogynic attitudes that they say continue to pervade many corporate suites. A common complaint among women officers, for instance, is that their duty is to write down decisions, not to make them.

The duties of Alice Bertrand, assistant secretary and an officer of Exxon Corp., are typical. Her responsibilities involve keeping the corporate records and notifying executives of management meetings. At these meetings, she sees that the items on the agenda are covered, and she takes notes.

"I don't have the right to participate in the discussion," she explains over lunch in Exxon's executive dining room—a privilege that came with the post and after 26 years of eating in the employes' cafeteria. "I only reflect the decisions and make sure the proper people are notified." Miss Bertrand says she isn't complaining, however; in fact, she says she is quite happy with her job and is pleased with the way Exxon has treated her.

In March 1973, Chrysler Corp. announced the appointment of its first woman clay modeler. On the one hand, the auto company hailed this event as a serious breakthrough. On the other hand, the release couched the appointment in terms of a society blurb rather than a straightforward business notice: "Strawberry blonde, blue-eyed Ginny Cartmell looks more like an artist's model than an artist or modeler. But her looks are deceiving. Ms. Cartmell is a clay modeler," the press release reads.

Ms. Cartmell's attitude toward her new job—which involves creating sculptural pieces from design sketches —"is as practical as the jeans and smock she works in," the release continues.

According to many businesswomen, such "slips" are commonplace. While men are considered intelligent and competent, the women say, executives assume women are neither. "You have to swallow a lot," says a manufacturing executive whose company's attitudes are still shaped by its bearded, dead founders. "I'm constantly asked if I'm 'one of those women libbers.' Immediately I feel I have to go into a 10-minute apologia for living."

In anticipation of such attitudes, most women in the management ranks tread very cautiously. They're careful not to show any emotional foible lest their colleagues label them "temperamental." They're careful to be low-key lest their subordinates think them "shrill."

"If you're timid, hesitant, or nervous, then you've confirmed the (female) stereotype," says Rita Hauser, a partner in the Wall Street law firm of Stroock & Stroock & Lavan. "That's the terror of it," she says. "Everybody has been shamed into having at least one woman as a director," Mrs. Hauser goes on, "but we haven't gotten beyond this first step. It's hard to break through to the second stage—that sex is irrelevant."

Under such strain, many women quit trying to climb the corporate ladder and just hang on. And this irks company officials who are under ever-increasing pressure to promote women but who don't want to promote women who are just hangers-on.

Indeed, some corporations are as unhappy about

the supply of promotable women as the women are about the opportunities for promotion. "There has been a void in women seeking the career opportunities we have to offer," says Clifford Merriott, director of news relations for General Motors Corp. (However, he says, GM "is really beginning to make significant progress in making women interested in engineering careers.")

In the meantime, many women, discouraged by the continued male dominance of the top corporations, now think more government action is needed to push corporations beyond what Mrs. Hauser calls the first step. (And at least some males agree. Says a male official at an insurance company: "Now it's women, before it was air pollution and before that the urban crisis. Some honest efforts are made, and then it's swept under the rug until the next crisis.")

Only a handful of firms initiated women's affirmative-action programs after the first Washington rumbling—in December 1971, when the Labor Department's "Revised Order 4" served notice on government contractors that they were required to initiate affirmative-action programs.

Other companies waited until the government showed more muscle. After the AT&T case, many companies began management-employment workshops to set up goals and timetables for hiring and promoting women. Still other firms moved in September 1973, when the EEOC notified General Motors, Ford Motor Co., General Electric Co. and Sears, Roebuck & Co. that charges of job discrimination had been filed against them.

That same month, for example, Massachusetts Mutual Life Insurance Co. officially geared up its affirmative-action program for women. As recently as 16 months before the program's official launching, the company automatically shuttled women off to clerical jobs while pushing men into its executive-training program. (A company official says that such a division of labor wasn't intentional. "Until our affirmative-action program, most of our recruiting was in the clerical area," he explains. "Now we're encouraging women to seek out positions as managers.")

One company, however, did move before governmental pressure. In January 1971, Dow Chemical Co. launched a program for advancing women through the ranks. Dow officials claim the impetus for the program came straight from top management—C. B. Branch, Dow's president, is the father of six daughters.

1974   MARY BRALOVE

Up-the-Ladder Blues

NEW England Telephone & Telegraph's top executives got a long letter from a young white male in middle management who complained that his future looked pretty dim because of the company's push to advance women and members of racial minorities into management slots. Are guys like him going to have "to pay for (this company's) discriminatory practices during the past century?" he asked. The top brass sent him a long-winded reply that boiled down to: Yes.

The young man is probably not the least comforted by the fact that a growing number of other white males are feeling the sting of de facto discrimination in hiring and promotion. "We found that white males are intensely angry—it's an Archie Bunker reaction, but it's real," says James B. Webber, a director of Cambridge Research Institute Inc. in Massachusetts, who is studying this emerging phenomenon.

Mr. Webber says the problem is just beginning to surface in such big companies as American Telephone & Telegraph, General Motors and Polaroid that are scrambling to meet the government's "affirmative-action goals"—which is the federal Equal Employment Opportunity Commission's (EEOC) jargon for hiring and promoting a certain number of nonwhites and women, or else. The "or else" could be severe. Companies want to avoid lawsuits like the one that led to

AT&T's landmark $15 million settlement in 1973 with employes who had charged discrimination had deprived them of past promotions and raises.

One large company is tired of "spending hundreds of thousands of dollars preparing, defending and losing" discrimination cases, its general counsel tells middle managers. "If you don't comply with the law (and promote women and minorities), you'll be fired."

Increasingly, however, white males are retorting that the law also forbids reverse discrimination. In fiscal 1973, ended June 30, more than 50 white males filed complaints with EEOC, charging firms with promotion discrimination, up from just three such complaints in fiscal 1968.

And, judging from corporate promotion plans, these complaints are likely to proliferate in coming years. AT&T says that by 1975 it will increase females in second-level management jobs by 33% and in upper-level jobs by 50%. GM says it is promoting one woman for every three men on most levels.

These moves will have an even greater impact on white males because the easing of overall corporate growth is expected to slow promotion rates in general during the 1970s. One firm that Mr. Webber has studied is growing at about 4.5% annually now, down from 8% in the 1960s, and its promotion rate will be five times less. Mr. Webber adds that lower retirement rates, a middle-management surplus and a trend to centralization will further reduce the room at the top.

Many companies deny they have a problem of white male backlash. "It's the exception rather than the rule," Frank Coss, executive vice president of Deutsch, Shea & Evans Inc., a New York consulting firm, says. "Does putting three women in a department of 150 really cause a problem?"

It does indeed. In anonymous interviews with 160

managers in a $2 billion company, Cambridge Research
Institute unearthed discontent on most levels, but primarily among managers just above the foreman level.
"This group was very specific about what EEOC means
to them. They see females who, they feel, aren't as
qualified as they could be, as slated for the opportunities," Mr. Webber says.

"That they feel there's no hope for them is a great
emotional shock," he says. "Some said they'd quit. Others said the company will drive out talent. One young
foreman said he's 'turned off' and won't work Satur-
days. A manager said he'd just 'do his job' and 'not
care.' "

Mr. Webber says the company's middle managers
cited top management's "commitment to the feds" and
said they "don't blame the younger guys" for leaving.
One divisional manager even advised his top engineer to
go elsewhere because he "didn't have a place for him,"
Mr. Webber says.

Eventually all this white-male resentment could
build up into a "motivational recession," affecting individual companies' progress and maybe even that of the
entire U.S. economy, Mr. Webber asserts. "We're just beginning to see it now, but the issue will soon become
crystallized, and companies must be prepared to meet
it," he says.

Few consultants or executives agree completely
with this assessment. "I see it as a tantrum, for heav-
en's sake—like saying if the game isn't stacked I won't
play," says Betsy Hogan, president of Betsy Hogan Associates, a Brookline, Mass., consulting firm that special-
izes in so-called affirmative-action problems. She thinks
white males are being treated fairly but that they think
it is unfair based on expectations of previous "privileged
treatment."

"They're in shock to think they'll have to compete

with three-fourths of the rest of the world as well, that they won't get brownie points for being white and male," she says. "Isn't a boy's final put-down the fact he got beaten by a girl?"

But the men who are complaining contend they are the victims of unfair competition, at best, and at worst, discrimination. One of these is Robert Currie, age 30, who was a mutual-fund manager at a Boston bank. He had seven years of financial experience, but he says he was passed over for an analyst's post in the bank's prestigious corporate-loan department in favor of an inexperienced female whom superiors deemed "qualifiable" if she enrolled in a program leading to a master of business administration degree.

"Promotions don't depend on ability, but on who you are," Mr. Currie says bitterly. "One just can't earn his way in a firm anymore." He quit because of the incident and now works for a management-consulting firm.

In Washington, D.C., a 25-year-old white male quit a television station when the producer-director job he was after went to a black trainee who didn't have as much experience and hadn't completed the station's training course. In another case, Polaroid promoted a college-educated female without experience in the specific area to a supervisory post over three experienced white males who didn't have degrees.

"I'm sure those men felt some resentment," says Susan Ells, Polaroid's senior equal-opportunity administrator. Like some others in the field, she thinks that "too many unqualified men reached the top in the past."

In any case, the criteriá that constitute qualification—such as requiring an MBA degree for admission to an elite management-training program—are rapidly changing. "Many past yardsticks had a disparate effect on women and minorities," says Ruth G. Shaeffer, senior specialist with Conference Board Inc., a New York business-research organization. "Today there's less emphasis on credentials and seniority, more on whether the individual can do the job," she says.

Whatever the criteria for hiring and promoting, the touchy question is: Are they being applied fairly to all concerned, or should they be bent in favor of minorities and women? This is the essence of a case before the U.S. Supreme Court, concerning a student who was twice denied admission to the University of Washington's law school while more than three dozen minority students with lower academic credentials were admitted. The issue—should the law school be allowed to give preferential treatment to minorities—has clear implications for businesses.

Meanwhile, companies are struggling to cope with enforced minority advancement on one hand and white-male backlash on the other. AT&T, for one, "first hit employes over the head with the law," but soon learned that was like hitting a large iron ball with a sledge-hammer—the ball moves but the hammer backfires," says John W. Kingsbury, assistant vice president of human resources development. Instead, Ma Bell changed its approach to "gentle, but consistent pressure," he says.

AT&T now makes a special effort to keep all employes fully informed about hiring and promotion policies by dispensing memos and TV tapes made by top executives, putting articles in house organs and manning hotlines for feedback.

GM's psychologist, Howard C. Carlson, who was given the job of preventing backlash from mushrooming, favors supervisors "actively listening" and "being honest" with disappointed young whites. In one case, he advised the supervisor to tell an upset young man "Look, I have to play catch-up."

Mr. Carlson is considering "some sort of general training" for bosses in this area, and has already embarked on a backlash prevention program that includes reviewing company policies and setting up workshops for personnel executives.

Mr. Webber of Cambridge Research Institute, however, thinks that dealing with backlash may require more radical approaches in the future. Many companies will have to devise new ways of motivating employes, he says.

His firm suggested several alternatives to the company it studied: earlier retirement, more lateral moves, a more horizontal rather than vertical organizational structure, and lengthy sabbaticals at part-salary. "What we're saying is that alternate social values may not be all that bad. People can relate to a company in other ways than 52 weeks a year," he says.

Richard E. Walton, director of the research division at Harvard University Graduate School of Business Administration, also suggests that companies de-emphasize up-the-ladder movement in favor of more horizontal moves to gain "valuable work experience." Some companies are beginning to implement such ideas. Many have sweetened voluntary early-retirement plans, and some, such as Xerox, offer employes time off to do alternate work.

1974   —LIZ ROMAN GALLESE

Men's Liberation

IT was a cause that was bound to gain momentum, and it has. Across the country, a group of oppressed people has begun to proclaim its rights vigorously and vociferously.

Their cause is known as "men's lib."

It's no joke. "Men's lib" has become a real cause, and it's gaining some real victories. Men from coast to coast say that they are being discriminated against by employers and others and the discrimination is illegal under the new laws that bar discrimination based on sex. The laws, of course, were designed to give women equal treatment, but the men say *they're* the ones who need the protection.

"It's about time we men got our rights," militantly asserts Robert H. Burns. "Fairness is fairness all around. Men can't be a doormat." Mr. Burns is a lawyer who represented a young man who applied for a job as steward with Pan American World Airways. Pan Am said its passengers prefer pretty girls and refused to hire the man. An appeals court ruled that Pan Am had violated civil rights sex discrimination laws by its all-female hiring policy. (Despite his tough talk, Mr. Burns works both sides of the street. He won the right for his cousin Barbara Jo Rubin to become a jockey.)

This case and others that are pending could prove significant—and costly—for American business. An engineer sued Illinois Bell Telephone Co. to force it to allow men to retire at age 55, when women can, rather than age 60, the minimum retirement age for men. As a result of the action, the Bell System adjusted its retirement policy to allow both men and women to retire at age 55. AT&T estimates the equal-treatment settlement boosts its annual pension costs by more than $50 million.

The U.S. Equal Employment Opportunity Commission has determined that a small-loan company's profit-sharing plan was discriminatory. It paid women their share any time they quit, but men got nothing unless they were at least 50 years old or disabled. The company vainly contended that women merited special treatment because their working careers were often shorter because of marriage or because their husbands were transferred out of town.

The Labor Department filed its first equal-pay case on behalf of men in August 1970. It sought higher pay for male teen-agers taking orders at two Illinois restaurants. The boys were getting less than women who were doing the same job. The case was settled when the restaurant owners agreed to raise the wages to the higher level.

Specialists in civil rights and labor matters say the issues are likely to increase and to become more complicated as more and more men realize that the sex discrimination laws work both ways. Some states provide minimum wages for women but not for men, says an official of the Equal Employment Opportunity Commission, and he sees these laws being challenged. Other states require employers to pay women for working overtime but say nothing about men who work more than 40 hours a week, he says. And he expects some men to demand the same meal and rest periods that women are allowed and to seek lounge facilities as nice as women's.

Men are using the legal ban on sex bias to pry open jobs previously limited to women. The first such case filed by a man with the New York City Commission on Human Rights involved an employment agency that had refused to refer him for a job. The agency claimed the employer wanted a female clerk, but the commission found its refusal discriminatory.

"You'll probably see more men coming forward with problems like that," says a spokesman for the New York commission. "If a man needs a job, he's going to press for it."

Some legal experts think that men will soon be coming forward with problems other than job discrimination. They say men are likely to challenge alleged discrimination in such areas as divorce law and property rights. Indeed, in 1970, a court in Waukesha, Wis., ordered a woman to pay $25 a week in child support to her former husband. He had been granted custody of their four children two years earlier, but he since had been laid off from his job at a machine tool shop.

But discrimination in employment will probably remain the chief battleground. Telephone companies across the nation have been under mounting pressure to hire men as well as women for jobs as operators. In some states, men are challenging hospital rules that bar the hiring of private duty male nurses for female patients, except on request; women nurses are routinely assigned to male patients, they note.

Men are also challenging — and sometimes overthrowing—rules that bar them from wearing long hair in their jobs. No such rules exist for women, they assert, and they want equal treatment. Thus, a challenged California employer has agreed to a single, unisexual standard "somewhere around the collar area," a Federal official says. Elsewhere, men have been allowed to keep jobs and their hair—if they agree to wear hairnets like those the women wear.

What do women think of all this talk about men's lib? Women militants, at least, say right on. "When laws are good laws, they should be applied to everyone," declares Lucy Komisar of the National Organization for Women. But adds, "If it's not a good law, it's probably used to keep women out of jobs."

1971   —JAMES C. HYATT

Expectant Mothers

BRIAN Smith doesn't look like the kind of kid to stir up a protest. At age 11 months, he's more engrossed in pulling himself up in his playpen than in pulling down established corporate custom.

But when Brian was born, his mother had to quit work without pay. She lost about $1,000 in wages, and she didn't like it. So 27-year-old Alberta Smith of Roanoke, Va., joined six other women workers and the International Union of Electrical Workers to sue General Electric Co. over policies at GE's Salem assembly plant. They charge that the company shows sex bias by refusing disability pay in maternity cases. "If a man hurt his finger, he'd get paid weekly disability benefits," Mrs. Smith complains.

As the challenge to GE indicates, women workers are taking up the cause of "maternity lib." They want to choose, without interference from the boss, when they'll quit work to have a baby and when they'll return. They want disability pay while unable to work. They seek more generous employer contributions for insurance covering their doctor and hospital bills. And they don't want an argument about getting their old job back when they return to work.

The battle rages on several fronts:

—In courtrooms, employers face government lawsuits alleging bias; Du Pont is accused on disability ben-

efits, National Can on leave policies. The Supreme
Court has overturned leave policies in Ohio and Virginia
schools, which required women to quit work early in
their pregnancies. And an Air Force captain who became pregnant is asking the Supreme Court to reverse
her discharge from the service.

—In union complaints to state and federal antibias agencies, a number of large corporations are being
accused of discrimination; many complaints assert that
sick-leave and disability benefits are available to men
for almost any reason but that maternity coverage for
women is barred.

In bargaining sessions, unions and women workers
are pushing for improved maternity leave, disability
pay and other benefits. Under such pressure, Polaroid
Corp., IBM and Cummins Engine Co. have all liberalized
policies; among others, Cummins now makes disability
payments in maternity cases. And many other firms are
reviewing their treatment of pregnant workers.

"Maternity lib" enjoys support from many women's
organizations. Groups ranging from the National Organization for Women (NOW) to the Business and Professional Women's Clubs to a Catholic antiabortion group
endorsed broader maternity benefits in a Wisconsin
hearing in 1972.

But to the amazement of many women, the issue
seems to generate much more business opposition than
do demands for equal pay and equal job opportunities.
"This is the hottest issue confronting personnel men
these days," asserts an official of the American Society
for Personnel Administration. An actuary for a leading
insurance firm adds: "This is a very emotional question."

Just the thought of paying for maternity time-off
repels some bosses. "There's a distinct difference between maternity and sickness, although that's almost

heresy as far as the Equal Employment Opportunity Commission is concerned," says James W. Hoose, director of industrial relations at Michigan Seamless Tube Co. "To pay a woman a salary during that period, when maternity is a matter of her choice, grates a little bit."

(Mrs. Smith, the GE worker, doesn't agree that maternity is purely a matter of choice. "Nobody is going out having babies to get a couple of pennies," she says. "Even with birth-control pills, women do get pregnant.")

And some employers worry that maternity disability benefits may be abused. They fear that doctors may be overly generous in certifying that a new mother is physically unable to return to work. Or they foresee that women will collect maternity disability checks and then quit work. "I'd imagine a number of employers would be looking closer at hiring women who've gone through the menopause," says one personnel man.

Much of the pressure for change comes from the Equal Employment Opportunity Commission in Washington. This four-man one-woman commission takes the position that any employment policy ought to apply equally to men and women. To provide for a male leg broken in a skiing accident while ignoring a temporarily disabled pregnant woman is absurd and unfair, according to the EEOC. In guidelines issued in 1972, it said pregnancy isn't a valid basis for refusing to hire, for discharging, laying off or denying promotions to women. For job purposes, the commission added, pregnancy, miscarriage, abortion, childbirth and recovery are "temporary disabilities and should be treated as such." The guidelines don't have the force of law, but the Supreme Court has indicated that it gives "great deference" to such administrative interpretations.

For employers, disability payments cause the deepest concern—and greatest potential cost. Companies often pay workers a percentage of their salary—70% is typical—when they're sick or injured and off the job. But most disability plans exclude or limit coverage for maternity. Even a generous plan may provide up to 26 weeks of disability pay for most injuries or illnesses but only six weeks for maternity.

The cost of maternity disability benefits, of course, depends on the number and age of women workers, the number of babies they have and the length of time that new mothers stay off the job. Adding six weeks of maternity coverage to a typical disability plan costs an extra 10% according to an official of Martin E. Segal Co., employe-benefit consultants. But one actuary estimates that in a group more than half female, maternity disability coverage lasting 26 weeks could increase premiums 80%.

General Electric estimates that providing up to 26 weeks of maternity disability payments could cost $4 million to $12 million a year, depending on actual usage; the company has more than 100,000 female workers. GE now pays up to 26 weeks of disability benefits at 60% of a worker's wage, up to a maximum of $150 a week, but it excludes maternity.

Perhaps significantly, the lawsuit against GE is pending before U.S. District Judge Robert R. Merhige Jr., who in 1971 ruled that the Chesterfield County, Va., school board couldn't require a teacher to quit after the fifth month of pregnancy; an appeals court upheld his decision. In a similar case the following year, two teachers won an appeals court finding that the Cleveland school system's maternity-leave policy discriminated against women. Pregnant teachers were required to take an unpaid leave five months before the birth of a child, and they couldn't return to work until the first school term after the child was three months old. Both courts said they found no medical justification for the rules. The Supreme Court has since upheld the rulings of the lower courts.

Outside the courts, equal-rights agencies are seeing an increasing number of maternity-related cases. Leave policies have been attacked in charges filed by the Communications Workers against AT&T, by the International Union of Electrical Workers against Westinghouse, and by the United Auto Workers against General Motors, Ford and Chrysler.

Under all this pressure, many employers are softening up on motherhood. A Prentice-Hall survey of 108 companies found more than half at least considering new policies as a result of the EEOC guidelines. A 1965 survey had found only one firm in five letting a pregnant employe decide when to quit working; the latest poll found six out of 10 firms leaving the decision to the worker and her physician.

National Broadcasting Co. has dropped a policy requiring a pregnant woman to quit in the seventh month and stay out three months after delivery. "Now she can go to the hospital right from work as long as the doctor approves," a spokesman says. "And if she can return the week after she delivers, terrific."

What's more important, more employers are offering disability benefits in maternity cases. In 1971 Cummins Engine made pregnancy a temporary disability for women, and union contracts negotiated the following year adopted the same change for other women employed by Cummins. The disability payments amount to "a couple of weeks at most in an uncomplicated pregnancy," an official says.

The Arma division of Ambac Industries Inc. in Garden City, N.Y., has proposed changing union contracts to include up to 26 weeks of maternity disability benefits. "We know the requirements relating to women are becoming more strict," says Mel Stebbins, manager of employe relations.

Such changes won't be enough to satisfy all the "maternity lib" demands. Pressure is expected, too, for bolder innovations, such as expansion of employer-paid hospital insurance to include maternity care for unmarried women. The EEOC guidelines have weakened corporate resistance to this step. In 1972, Blue Cross of Northeast Ohio offered holders of group policies a rider for single-person maternity coverage. "A dozen groups have enrolled," an official reports. "Companies think they're going to be under the gun eventually, and they're getting an early jump."

Other possible pattern-setters can be glimpsed now. The Delevan division of American Precision Industries, in East Aurora, N.Y., negotiated a liberalized leave late in 1971 for mothers of newly adopted children. The policy permits a six-month leave, without pay and without loss of seniority, when a child is adopted; previously, only a one-month leave was permitted.

And in contract talks between the professional staff and City University of New York, the university has proposed formal leave policies for faculty members that could include paid "paternity leave" for new papas needed at home.

1972   —JAMES C. HYATT

Part-Time Professionals

FRANCES Loughran was caught in a dilemma: After 20 years of marriage and child rearing, she yearned to take advantage of her previous training as a psychologist.

"At the same time, I didn't want a job that wouldn't leave me with the time necessary for my family," says Mrs. Loughran, who lives in Westchester County, N.Y., with her husband and eight children.

She solved her problem by landing a part-time job as a market researcher with Educational Records Bureau, a New York company that does testing for private schools. "I get a sense of satisfaction by working as a professional, yet my hours are flexible enough that I have time for the rest of my life," says Mrs. Loughran, who holds a master's degree in psychology from Fordham University.

Such a solution isn't unique. A growing number of women, who want to utilize their professional backgrounds but who don't want careers that could consume most of their time and energy, are looking for stimulating part-time work. And employers, noting this previously untapped reservoir of womanpower, are finding a surprising array of jobs, ranging from managing offices to editing and legal work, that can be handled by women on a part-time basis.

Until recently, the idea of hiring anyone as part-time professionals or managers—other than using the knowledge of consultants and, in some cases, retirees—was avoided as being too disruptive to work routine and simply causing administrative headaches. Lately, however, employers are finding out that "the woman with a professional background but who can't work full-time because of home responsibilities often works out better than regular employes," says Peter Powers, general counsel for the Smithsonian Institution, who has two part-time women attorneys on his staff.

Others agree. United Publishing Corp. of Washington, for instance, used 54 part-timers (all women) among the 200 writers and researchers who put together its "New American Encyclopedia." Grayson & Associates, an Englewood, N.J., marketing concern, has a female office manager who works about 25 hours a week. And the Atomic Energy Commission has at least one part-time professional—a female physicist—on the payroll.

"I prefer working with part-time women. The mind doesn't have to be in an office 40 hours a week to be creative, and many women seem to put in a lot more time thinking about their job than the number of hours they get paid for it," says Allan Kulen, vice president of United Publishing. Besides, he says, the company doesn't have to pay fringe benefits to part-timers; these usually lift labor costs by at least 6% above salaries.

Peter Lewis, president of Progressive Insurance Co., Cleveland, is also staunchly pro part-timers. He says that after experiencing the enthusiasm of women clerks working part-time, he's going to begin hiring females as claims adjusters, underwriters and "the entire gamut of managerial positions." He adds: "I'm convinced we will be able to structure a work schedule permitting women to be on five-hour shifts. Why not use these talented, motivated and well-educated people?"

Not everyone shares that attitude. The trend thus far appears limited primarily to small companies that are perhaps more flexible in their personnel policies because of relatively limited number of employes. Then again, some employers fear working mothers—whether full-time of part-time—will miss more time than co-workers because of sick children or other problems that could crop up at home. Also, some women claim "male chauvinism" is still a strong deterrent to hiring women in a part-time capacity for other than clerical or manual jobs.

"There's still tremendous resistance by many company officials to scheduling shorter hours for women," complains Vickie Kramer, who works with Options for Women, Philadelphia, one of a mounting number of organizations trying to get companies to loosen up their policies regarding "short-shift" women. "It's a gut reaction to thinking their wives might dare to go out and do a job similar to theirs on a part-time basis."

A good many husbands, though, apparently find their wives' jobs more therapeutic than threatening. "I think it's great. Working has improved my wife's frame of mind quite a bit. And it's good for the children not to depend on her all the time," says Jim Malaro, a physicist at the Atomic Energy Commission. His wife, Marie, is one of the Smithsonian's part-time lawyers. (Mr. Malaro himself works with the AEC's part-time female physicist.)

"Women usually aren't working part-time just to help support the family. Work is simply an important part of their lives. But you have to convince the top brass of companies that that's the case," says Fran Goldman, a founder of Distaffers, a Washington agency similar to Options for Women. (Mrs. Loughran, for instance, used her first paycheck from Education Records Bureau to buy a painting she long admired.)

Some steps are being taken, though, to get the women's cause into the executive suite. Catalyst, a nationwide women's educational organization based in New York, received grants totaling $300,000 from the Kellogg, Ford and Rockefeller foundations to draw up a progam for the employment of well-educated women on a less than full-time basis.

To show the value of part-time women, Catalyst points to a study it made in 1971 of 50 women working half-time as case-workers in Boston with the state department of welfare. The study shows the women actually had more face-to-face contact with the people they were aiding than did regular employes, they carried slightly more than half the case load of the full-timers, and their turnover rate was significantly below that of full-time case-workers.

Despite progress made thus far, however, those seeking more part-time professional jobs for women say that steps toward their goal are a good bit daintier than they would like. The major obstacle that must be overcome, they say, is getting giant employers, including the federal government, to pursue actively the hiring of women professionals on a part-time level. (In 1967, John D. Gardner, then head of the Department of Health Education and Welfare, initiated a project to attract women to part-time career jobs with the agency. When he resigned a year later, however, the program fizzled out.)

"The government is just one big employer that's ignorant of a lot of talent under its nose," says Felice Schwartz, Catalyst's president.

1972   —GAIL BRONSON

No-Account Females

ESTELLE G. Antell, a federal employe in Dallas, would appear to be an ideal airline customer. Her income is around $20,000 a year, and she flies at least 100,000 miles annually. Thus, she didn't expect any problems in 1971 when she moved to Dallas from Tulsa and applied to Continental Air Lines for a credit card in her own name.

"Back came a letter asking for my husband's signature," she says. "I called up and said, 'You've got to be kidding. How many men in my wage bracket do you ask for the wife's signature?' " She never received the card. And the final insult came recently "when a Continental salesman came by asking why I didn't fly Continental. You can bet I told him."

As Mrs. Antell's experience indicates, many women are finding that liberation hasn't pervaded all segments of the business world. Banks, savings and loan institutions, department stores and other firms that extend credit frequently are reluctant to let an employed married woman do business in her own name. Many widowed or divorced women find the problems become even more troublesome. And for young married couples the wife's income often carries little or no weight in such vital transactions as securing a home mortgage.

Thus, the effort to weed sex discrimination out of the credit card and the loan office is becoming yet another major front in the women's equality battle. Department stores increasingly are finding themselves subject to picketing and account cancellations over their credit practices. [In 1973, the Senate passed an amendment to the Truth in Lending Act prohibiting discrimination in credit practices on the basis of sex or marital status. Similar legislation is being considered by a House subcommittee.]

"Men and women today don't have equal access to credit," Martha W. Griffiths, Congresswoman from Michigan, has testified. "Banks, savings and loan associations, credit-card companies, finance companies, insurance companies, retail stores and even the federal government discriminate against women in extending credit. And they discriminate against women in all stages of life—whether single, married, divorced or widowed; with or without children, rich or poor, young or old."

She was a witness at hearings in 1972 before the National Commission on Consumer Finance, a government agency. The testimony indicated "the reasoning used to deny women credit is often a cobweb of myths and suppositions unsupported by research on the statistical risks involved or on the individual's credit-worthiness," Virginia H. Knauer, special assistant to the President for consumer affairs, told the International Consumer Credit Conference in Washington in 1972.

Some examples cited:

—A regularly employed woman in her early 30s couldn't get a loan to purchase a vacation home although she could make a substantial down payment. Her fiance, who had been through bankruptcy, easily obtained a loan to purchase the same property with a smaller down payment.

—A woman in her 40s who, as head of her household, wanted to buy a house for herself and her children couldn't get a mortgage without the signature of her 70-year-old father, who was living on a pension.

—A woman widowed for six years found it easier to open charge accounts in her dead husband's name than in her own.

—As a condition to being granted a mortgage, a couple in Washington was asked by a bank "to agree in writing not to have a child for a specified period of time." Another lender wanted a doctor's assurance that "a proper method of birth control was being used or, in the alternative, that the woman wasn't fertile."

Companies and financial institutions contend that such examples aren't typical, and they note with some irony that not so long ago they were being criticized for wide distribution of unsolicited credit cards. "You didn't hear the women complaining then," says one official in the consumer credit industry. Nonetheless, many credit grantors concede their credit policies concerning women are under considerable pressure and are frequently being changed.

Some find the problem is getting the word of top-level policy down to the rank and file. Thus, Continental Air Lines says if Mrs. Antell, the Dallas woman, was turned down in spite of a clear credit record, "we made a mistake. Our policy is to treat applicants as individuals. Tell her to refile."

Ironically, working married women who established a credit standing when they were single often appear to have the most difficulty. "You lose your credit when you marry," says Marsha King, president of the Texas division of Women's Equity Action League (WEAL), a nationwide women's group. When she married and set about changing the name on her credit cards, she found Dallas retailers reluctant.

"I had excellent credit and had done a lot of business. But they told me I'd have to reapply in my husband's name," she says. The demand was particularly irksome, she says, because "I have always paid all the bills in the family. I don't know of anyone who has ever received a check from my husband."

Working married women who are supporting an unemployed husband—a student, for instance—often find their credit status different from that of a man supporting his nonworking wife. In 1972, for example, the St. Paul human-rights department sent a man and a woman separately to 23 area banks to borrow $600 for a used car.

Each was earning $12,000 a year and was the sole support of a family with almost identical financial and personal qualifications. But about half the banks applied more stringent standards to the woman than to the man, the researchers found. These banks refused to lend the woman money without her husband's signature while waiving the co-signature requirement for the man, for instance.

Following the survey, department officials told the banks their policies appeared to be in violation of the city's antidiscrimination ordinance. "We came up with an agreement that they wouldn't require any more from a woman than a man. They're even rewriting their forms to say spouse instead of wife," says Louis Ervin, director of the department.

Some women are particularly irritated that companies freely let husbands speak for the wife in financial transactions but don't give wives the same privilege. Consider, for instance, the Louisiana woman who discovered that her husband had opened up a stock-trading account in her name at an office of a major brokerage house. "The broker apparently was glad to do it, so long as my husband would co-sign," she says. The husband filled out the application, but the wife was never consulted by the brokerage house.

Then the husband began actively trading in the account, and often he transferred funds from "her" account to his. "He generally just manipulated the situation, and they never once had my signature, or any contact with me," says the woman.

When she finally learned about the account, she called the brokerage firm. "Do I have an account at your office?" she asked. " 'Oh, yes,' they said. 'But your husband always does your business.' I said I'd never done any business with them, and they'd better find a way to indicate that on their records." For some weeks, when she called, the brokerage firm told her the account was still open. Recently, she says, "they've been saying the right words. They tell me I have no account up there. I really don't know if they're just telling me that." (So why hasn't she left her husband? "I can't, for financial reasons," she says. "You can say I live with my husband, but it is an awfully big house.")

Married women say opening new credit accounts in their own name, even when they are employed, is often a problem. In 1971, Mrs. Vee Carlock, a legal secretary in Baton Rouge, ordered a $500 refrigerator at her local Sears store. She planned to pay the bill when the item was delivered.

At the store, however, she decided to take a service contract, which cost $54, and she asked to open a charge account in her own name. "The clerk started explaining that it is illegal in Louisiana to extend credit to a woman. I said I know that isn't the law. I talked to two or three clerks, and finally the credit manager. I kept telling them I work, I earn more than my husband and I'm perfectly capable of paying my bills.

"After two hours of haggling, it was close to closing time, and I said, 'Let's just forget the whole purchase.' So the manager said, 'Well, we will open the account if you insist!' When he found out I was only charging

$54, he almost had a stroke." Ironically, she never received her refrigerator; the store couldn't fill the order, and she bought it at another store where she had had an account for several years.

(At the 1972 Washington hearings, officials from Sears testified that while the company prefers to open only one account per family, a wife meeting normal credit standards could get her own account. It isn't in Sears' best interest, they added, "to turn customers away from its doors.")

Frustrated by credit problems, women are resorting to a number of tactics. Picketing, refusal to accept credit cards in their husbands' names, and general complaining have led to some changes in department store policies in Chicago and Syracuse, women say. Lynne Litwiller, who heads a task force on credit problems for the National Organization for Women, says that while many retailers routinely will turn down a woman's credit request, "if she calls the credit manager and puts up a big fuss, more and more stores will give credit in her own name. But the stores really don't like to do it. It still hasn't been established as a right."

Other women are considering lawsuits against lenders, although the legal grounds appear far from certain. No state or federal laws appear to directly ban sex discrimination in credit transactions. Attorneys working with the women's movement say lawsuits in the works involve instances such as stores persisting in sending bills to a husband although the goods were ordered in the wife's name, a case involving two women veterinarians who have been turned down for bank loans while younger, less experienced men vets have easily borrowed money, and a case where a bank giving men employes of a major industry a particularly favorable interest rate has refused to give the same rate to women workers whose husbands are employed else-where.

In response, lenders often acknowledge that their policies are undergoing constant review, but they caution that the women's demands often ignore real risks in granting credit. "More attention will have to be given to this area of lending in the future," says William E. Jones, vice president of consumer loans at City National Bank, Columbus, Ohio. The bank is a noted marketing innovator. "More women are working than ever before," he says. "More young people are wanting money. Banks have got to be prepared to extend credit to that class of people. We're all learning our lesson on that one every day."

Indeed, he concedes that while City National will give married women their own BankAmericard if they have their own income and a good credit record, "that wasn't the policy when we started the card six years ago." But he stresses that a young woman borrower in the child-bearing age raises questions for credit men. "Betting on her to be able to work every day for the next four years isn't the same as betting on a man," he asserts. "It is impossible to put a man and a woman on the same level completely as far as extending credit is concerned."

At the Washington hearings, John P. Farry, president of the U.S. Savings and Loan League, said "there has been a substantial reshaping of our thinking with respect to real-estate credit involving women." A survey covering 421 S&Ls indicates "that it is fast becoming much easier for a woman to get a mortgage," he said. Most of the institutions said they've liberalized policies toward giving credit to working wives in making mortgage loans.

Clearly some lenders are losing business due to stringent policies in that area. When Bob and Carol

Wellman, a Cleveland couple, asked Park View Federal Savings & Loan for a home loan, they were told the firm wouldn't consider her income in the application. So the couple took their proposition to Cleveland Trust Co., where they got the loan when they assured the lending officer they had no plans to start a family any time soon.

An officer at Park View says that to consider a wife's income when a young couple has no children "does us a disservice and them a disservice," for when they start a family "then they are stuck and she has no income."

1972   —JAMES C. HYATT

Take a Letter

SITUATED in several elegant brick townhouses in the fashionable Back Bay area of Boston, the Katharine Gibbs School teaches a would-be executive secretary everything she has to know about pleasing her future boss, who is always a "him."

Helen Cole, the well-tailored acting director of the 550-student school, tells students that their ultimate objective as secretaries is to free up their boss's time "and let him get into creative things or research." One class of executive secretaries is cautioned never to allow their bosses to tamper with files. "Impress upon him that he's so important he shouldn't file," a teacher says. "He'll never file it back right."

Women's liberation may be gaining in popularity, but the six Katharine Gibbs schools endure as bastions of submissive femininity. Despite talk about expanded job opportunities for women, the chain is thriving as never before with its time-tested formula of typing, shorthand and personal grooming. Enrollment climbed to 2,500 in 1974 from 1,900 in 1971 and its graduates continue to be among the most sought-after secretaries around.

The schools have been a big hit almost from the day Katharine Gibbs, a widow, opened the first one in Providence back in 1911. (She had only one student at the beginning.) In 1917 she opened a school in Boston and a year later, another in New York. The chain was acquired in 1968 by Macmillan Inc., the New York publishing firm, and since 1971 has undergone its biggest growth since the early days. New schools have been opened in Huntington, N.Y., and Norwalk, Conn., and more are being contemplated. (The sixth school is in Montclair, N.J.) Since its founding, the chain figures it has turned out about 55,000 secretaries.

Why would a liberated generation of young women still come to Katy Gibbs, as the schools are known to students and alumni? Because, Gibbs officials say, most businesses are still primarily interested in hiring women to do the typing and shorthand. According to Edith Gardner, executive vice president of the chain, while men are frequently given on-the-job training, businesses typically ask women, "What can you do right now?"

Katherine Davis, a 22-year-old graduate of Colorado Women's College in Denver, found this to be the case. She got a bachelor's degree in European history in 1973 after four years of study and an investment of about $17,000. But no job offers awaited her. So now she's shelling out nearly another $5,000 for a year of postgraduate study at the Katharine Gibbs school in Boston.

While women with college degrees who can't type or take shorthand pound the pavement in search of jobs, the average Gibbs graduate can expect to choose from about four job offers, each paying an average of about $130 a week, Gibbs officials say. Gibbs graduates are in demand not only because of a chronic secretarial shortage, but because Gibbs has a nationwide reputation in the business world for turning out supersecretaries. "They're very well-trained and have a definite finishing touch," says Barbara O'Connor, employment services supervisor at New England Mutual Life Insurance Co., Boston. Gibbs grads are the firm's largest single source of new secretaries, she says.

Students can enroll at Gibbs straight out of high school, although more than 25% enter the Boston and New York schools with two or more years of college. Admission is competitive, Gibbs officials say, and is based on past academic record, references and an entrance exam. The chain estimates about 20% of its applicants are rejected. The school advertises in women's magazines like Seventeen, but figures the bulk of its students come because of its wide reputation or family tradition. "My mother went to Gibbs, and I've heard about it for years," says Miss Davis.

The school's finishing-school atmosphere and considerable tuition have traditionally attracted a well-heeled student body. In the early 1930s, Gibbs held March and April classes in Bermuda for girls who could afford it. That ended when the Depression deepened, but now tuition is a steep $1,860, and room and board (available only at the Boston school) runs another $2,650.

Full-time students sign up for either a one-year secretarial program or a two-year program that also includes some liberal-arts courses. Gibbs also offers evening secretarial courses and, a few years ago, started an intensive eight-week course for college graduates who want to learn basic typing and shorthand skills to improve their job chances.

The Gibbs approach to education survives as an anachronism that would warm the heart of the most demanding male chauvinist. Although the schools are ostensibly open to both sexes, only one male student has ever enrolled full-time, and students are known as "Gibbs Girls."

Except for a declining emphasis on accounting in favor of more administrative secretarial duties, the Gibbs curriculum is virtually unchanged from its earliest days. In courses covering all facets of officework, students learn different filing methods, practice telephone responses and are taught to make travel arrangements for their bosses. In one "Secretarial Procedures" course they learn the difference between special-handling and special-delivery mail and the number of time zones in the United States.

Along with typing, shorthand and filing, Gibbs emphasizes basics like posture and hand care. In a lecture on proper grooming, students are told to use deodorant, brush their teeth and be sure not to wear torn or ill-fitting underwear. "Get yourself together underneath," admonishes the impeccably groomed teacher. "We here at Katharine Gibbs are trying to make you into a pretty package," she adds. "You should blend into the office background so your boss can be proud of you." (But not too far into the background. The class is also advised: "If you have a nice bust, wear your pins toward the bust or cleavage. Heck, if you've got it, flaunt it.")

Although the hats and white gloves that were an essential part of student attire until the mid-1960s have been dropped, Gibbs retains an aura of genteel propriety. Men are barred beyond the lounge of its Boston dormitory, and students are still sent home from classes for failure to wear either dresses, skirts or color-coordinated slack outfits, as well as stockings and elevated-heel shoes.

The prim code of conduct and exacting standards are largely a legacy from Mrs. Gibbs' days at the helm. "We like to see things done nicely and done well," Mrs. Cole says. Schedules are rigorous; students attend classes from 9 a.m. to 3 p.m. and are expected to study and practice their typing and shorthand another two to three hours a day. Students must sit in alphabetical order in class and are forbidden to talk in the halls after a shorthand test, lest the next class get an inkling of what's to come. Instructors, ever formal, always address students as Miss or Mrs., never by their first name. When typing letters, students aren't allowed to use correction paper to rub out mistakes, on the theory that they will simply be repeating errors. A single instance of incorrect punctuation, misspelling or word division at the end of a line in a typed letter renders it unmailable and elicits a failing mark.

"A Gibbs graduate really knows how to cross her T's and dot her I's," says Edna Weathers Dennis, Gibbs' marketing manager. But for some of the students who have already been to college, the strict atmosphere is oppressive. "They treat you like you're 13," says Joan Fireman, a 21-year-old student who had nearly three years of college before coming to Gibbs.

Gibbs veterans contend, though, that the rules are downright lax compared to earlier years. Until the mid-1960s, for instance, students weren't allowed to wear head scarves or leave the dorm in shorts unless they wore raincoats over them. Students caught chewing gum in class were fined 25 cents. And after long hair became popular with girls in the late 1960s, Gibbs for several years insisted that its students wear their hair no longer than collar level.

The topic of women's liberation lurks only dimly in the background at Gibbs. In 1969, about 50 women invaded the chain's New York headquarters protesting that Gibbs teaches women to be subservient to men. And a Boston teacher says a student once protested being told in a grooming class that women should keep their legs and underarms shaved.

But according to one instructor, "All the students care about is what they're going to do next weekend." Students don't dispute that. "One Friday night there were 11 parties going on," says Sally Jo Ward, a black-haired student. "It was great." And Miss Davis, the Colorado Women's College graduate, says of the women's liberation movement: "I have no interest in it."

Gibbs is quick to point out that despite its old-fashioned approach, it encourages women to try to rise beyond secretarial jobs. Half its own top officers are women, it notes, and some of its graduates have gone far in the business world. A favorite example is Janet Lohmann Wortmann, a 1958 Gibbs graduate who worked her way up from secretary to assistant vice president and highest-ranking woman at Kidder, Peabody & Co., a brokerage firm. Of the school, Mrs. Wortmann says, "I owe them a lot for giving me a basic tool to work with."

Gibbs has begun offering special evening management-training courses for women. They carry such titles as "Essentials of Financial Planning" and "Supervisory and Managerial Techniques," but they have yet to win from employers anything approaching the accolades awarded the secretarial courses. Polaroid Corp., for instance, which has one of the most liberal employe-education plans in industry, refuses to grant its usual education allowance to employes wishing to take the Gibbs management courses. "No one at Gibbs can explain what students do except sit in a group," says Susan Ells, who is charged with evaluating outside courses at Polaroid.

The fact that Katharine Gibbs was the first to teach women such things as accounting and grammar in addition to typing and shorthand qualifies her as "one of the original women's libbers," Miss Gardner says. At the time Mrs. Gibbs opened her Providence school, both men and women did clerical work. But women were usually assigned the more menial tasks and were themselves known as "typewriters." Mrs. Gibbs felt women could do more in the office, such as compose letters and make various decisions for their bosses.

Ironically, Mrs. Gibbs wasn't much good at typing or shorthand and never worked as a secretary, according to her son, Gordon Gibbs, retired president of the chain. She was a forceful businesswoman, though, and her timing was right. As men went off to fight World War I, women were pushed into more responsible clerical positions and her schools prospered.

After Mrs. Gibbs died in 1934, the chain remained in her family until it was acquired by Macmillan. A spokesman for Macmillan won't specify the chain's revenues or profits but says both have shown "an upward trend" since the acquisition. Prior to that, the schools were "tremendously profitable," Mr. Gibbs says.

1974   —David Gumpert

Awareness Can Help

IT was a mortifying experience for everyone concerned.

As a top New York insurance executive recalls it, his company stood to lose the account of a sizable corporate customer unless certain sticky problems could be hashed out. Preparing for a long grueling session in the customer's office, he handed a nearby woman several dollars and told her to run out and bring back coffee for everyone. She refused, icily informing him that she was the company's general counsel. It was all downhill after that, and the insurer was not surprised that he lost the account.

He shakes his head now and comments, "I should have known better. One of our own attorneys is a woman."

Pure male chauvinism? Hardly. Like many businessmen he suffered from lack of awareness of a potential pitfall that's becoming more and more common as an increasing number of women move into responsible business positions. In fact, veteran businesswomen trained in a male business world sometimes make similar slips in their dealings with other businesswomen.

We're not talking here about the bigger issues of equal pay for women or equal job opportunities, but the sticky smaller problems that at first glance may seem petty. They aren't, at least to women trying to perform effectively on an equal basis in the business world.

Put yourself, for example, in the place of a financial reporter for this publication who recently met five high-level executives for lunch at the Marco Polo Club in the Waldorf Astoria Hotel in New York. They had arrived early and been served drinks when she arrived—setting off fireworks. Women weren't allowed in the Marco Polo at lunch, attendants said. So the entire group, drinks and all, had to troop downstairs to the public Bull and Bear Restaurant.

Embarrassing? Perhaps nearly as much for her as for the president of the company who had set up the lunch.

Most women in business have collected a plethora of such mini-horror stories. Some businessmen, on the other hand, are struggling with such issues as whether or not to light a businesswoman's cigaret, apparently in dread fear of being branded a "male chauvinist pig."

In an effort to bring a little order to this confusion, more than 20 businesswomen—ranging from securities analysts to the president of an advertising agency—were asked for pointers to steer well-meaning executives away from the most common pitfalls. Here they are.

1. Don't assume a woman contacted in business or over a business phone is a receptionist or secretary—even if she answers a man's telephone. She may be his boss.

2. Avoid calling women "sweetie," "honey," or "dear," unless you're comfortable calling male business executives "buddy-boy," "pal" or "chum." If you do that, you probably aren't reading this anyway.

3. As for lighting cigarets, opening doors or helping with coats (or even telling off-color stories and using swear words, for that matter) do whatever comes most naturally. None of the women cared one way or the other, as long as men don't make a big production of it.

But women see red when a man accompanies a light with a comment such as, "I hope you aren't one of those women's libbers." If she opposed such things, she would have met your light with a simple refusal.

In fact, while a number of women executives keep up with the women's liberation movement, few are chip-on-the-shoulder militants. The entire topic of women's liberation is best left out of day-to-day business dealings, relegated off-limits with politics and religion. Businesswomen also don't appreciate a case-by-case description of every female clerk your company has promoted to executive assistant. They'd much rather get to the business at hand.

4. Avoid private clubs when you're setting up a luncheon or gathering that will include women, unless you're absolutely certain women have equal access to club facilities, as they now do at Manhattan's Lawyers Club, which has recently moved to total male-female integration.

This can be tricky. For example, while New York's Union League Club will assure you on the phone that women guests are now permitted, club personnel frequently forget to mention that women are relegated to a separate "ladies" entrance and elevator. To make matters worse, when a women tries to leave by the League's second floor "ladies" elevator, which adjoins the kitchen, she runs into more difficulties. It doesn't appear to have a button. (Actually it's usually hidden behind movable paneling.)

Many clubs have separate "ladies" dining rooms for groups that include women, which is annoying enough. The Bankers Club in New York, which has its "ladies" dining room on the 38th floor, has its only women's bathroom on the 40th.

If a problem does develop, such as a group ouster from a private club, a woman appreciates a man's following her lead. If she tries to ignore the slight, brush the incident aside. But if she's clearly annoyed, back her up when possible. And a particularly thoughtful gesture is a letter of complaint to the management or individual involved, with a carbon to the businesswoman.

5. As for who pays the lunch tab, leave the decision to the business situation. Don't battle for the bill when lunching with an advertising executive who's trying to sell you a new campaign just because she's a woman. Her company expects her to pay. And don't make an issue of how uncomfortable this makes you. It shouldn't.

6. In addressing a letter to a woman, Ms. is acceptable to most businesswomen, unless they've indicated otherwise in their own correspondence. Some people do feel that Ms., pronounced miz, has an uncomfortable hayseed sound when spoken. None of the married women polled object to orally being called Miss, or Mrs. if you're certain they're married. But all objected to men making a big issue of it.

One advertising executive has a vivid mental picture of a marketing vice president who met her at the door with an enormous leer, slurping, "What shall we call you dear, Miss or Mizzzzzzz?"

7. Avoid sending out formal invitations to a businessman "and wife." It's as easy to engrave them with "and spouse" and even "and friend or guest," particularly if some of the invited guests are women.

8. When meeting with an executive group that includes one woman, don't automatically assign her the task of note-taking, assuming she takes shorthand.

9. Equally annoying to women executives are men who lapse into patronizing explanations. Assume a businesswoman is intelligent and knows her job unless she demonstrates otherwise. The company probably

wouldn't have made her their treasurer if she didn't know long division.

10. Avoid calling your secretary "my girl," or asking other executives—particularly in memos—to "have your gals" do something or other. If your company's secretaries and clerks are all women, and executives are all men, they probably shouldn't be. And anyway, the inference of ownership is demeaning. And if there are women executives and male clerks such comments are a slap.

These pointers won't be much use to businessmen who are truly opposed to women in business, or who operate from deep prejudice. But far more common is simple blindness to the entry of women into the real business world.

The St. Paul Companies, an insurance complex based in Minnesota, devoted almost all of its 1971 annual shareholder report to a proud recital of the progress of women in the company.

But temporary blindness resulted in the paradoxical inclusion of two final pages showing photos of the company's top executives—all men.

Awareness can help.

1973   —PRISCILLA S. MEYER

Feminist Entrepreneurs

THE hiring practices at Diana Press Inc. are downright discriminatory, and co-founder Coletta Reid doesn't care who knows it. "Men don't touch any job that we do," she boasts. "Our goal is to help other women."

A Baltimore-based publishing and printing concern owned and operated by women, Diana Press not only shows male job applicants the door, it refuses to accept male customers. (Its owners say they have more business than they can handle from women.) The company's avowed aim—besides making a profit—is to promote the feminist cause and bring more women into business at all levels.

As such, Diana Press has much in common with a host of new feminist businesses that have come into being since the women's liberation movement began to gather steam in the late 1960s. These companies range from personnel-placement and management-counseling services to manufacturing concerns turning out everything from male-chauvinist-pig pincushions to aprons for women who hate housework.

Precise statistics on the number of companies founded or acquired by female entrepreneurs aren't available. But their ranks are swelling. "The New Woman's Survival Catalog," a directory of firms serving the feminist market, lists more than 500 such companies. The Center for Venture Management, a nonprofit Milwaukee organization that studies small businesses, reports a sudden surge in the number of women attending its seminars on how to start a business. "It used to be there were only wives with their husbands," says director John Komives. "Now they're women on their own." Generally small in size, the new feminist businesses are scattered from coast to coast and exist mainly by buying and selling to one another.

"What we're seeing is the first step in an evolutionary process," says Lawrence C. Hackamack, a small-business specialist at Northern Illinois University in De Kalb, Ill., who compares the businesswomen to earlier generations of immigrants starting out in American society. "Like the Italians and Greeks, the women are selling first just to their own people," he says. As they get more experience, he predicts, they will follow historical precedent and expand into more extensive markets.

According to observers like Prof. Hackamack, the rising number of female-owned businesses reflects the degree of cynicism many women feel about their chances for success in conventional male-dominated corporations. Indeed, many of the feminist entrepreneurs say the main reason they cut loose from traditional jobs was a belief that they were being barred from advancement because of their sex. "Basically, we found that we couldn't get anywhere as women," says Stephanie L. Marcus, who teamed up with Rose Fontanella, another commercial artist, to found Liberation Enterprises, a Brooklyn, N.Y., novelty concern.

Though few of the companies with a niche in the feminist economy are making it big, some are well on the way. The most visible of these successful enterprises is Ms. magazine, a monthly serving as advertising medium, market research arm and cheering section for the women's movement. Ms. had a head start, being better capitalized than perhaps any other firm in the feminist market. In addition to a number of individual investors,

Warner Communications Inc., New York, agreed to invest up to $1 million in Ms. in return for a 25% ownership. Actually, Ms. needed only about half that much before becoming profitable. Patricia Carbine, publisher and editor-in-chief, says Ms. became profitable less than a year after the first issue appeared in mid-1972. Since then, profits have been steadily improving, she says, although she declines to give specific figures.

Flush with success, Ms. officials are planning a series of new projects to boost profits further. A new division is being created to make the magazine's expertise in the feminist market available for a fee to other concerns. In addition, Ms. is sounding out insurance companies about possibly offering policies to readers. And, it is considering a joint venture in the toy business, a movie and a radio show.

Ms. has such influence among feminists that an ad placed in it or a passing mention in an article is enough to produce a financial windfall for small companies. Liberation Enterprises was limping along until an article appeared in Ms. describing how it was founded. Besides producing an avalanche of orders, the article prompted a flood of fan mail from women who had been inspired to start their own businesses. Pat Windle, co-owner of Those Uppity Women, a jewelry concern in Indialantic, Fla., says, "Right around the time of the month that Ms. comes out, our business surges up to $300 a day for about a week." Normally, she says, the company's sales run around $75 to $80 a day.

What sets many of the feminist concerns apart from conventional businesses is their dedication to politics as well as profits. "We feel very strongly that we're serving the women's movement," declares Stephanie L. Marcus of Liberation Enterprises.

Scores of the newly formed businesses are supporting the movement with more than just good intentions.

Editors of the fast-selling "New Woman's Survival Catalog," for instance, have pledged a minimum of 20% of the book's royalties to the feminist cause. Similarly, Those Uppity Women promises in its ads to plow back 10% of its profits to women's rights groups.

Strong commitment to the principles of women's liberation lead feminist enterprises to seek out the services of other such concerns. For example, many feminist businesses plan to use First Women's Bank and Trust Co., a New York bank organized by women that has received preliminary approval from state regulatory authorities. "We plan to give women the kind of credit they would get if they were men," says Sarah Kovner, one of the organizers. "Credit won't necessarily be any easier, it will just be credit like men can get at other banks," she says. The stick-together philosophy motivated Lammas Arts & Crafts, a Washington, D.C., concern run by women, to hire a feminist accountant and a feminist lawyer. And, while New Feminist Talent Associates, a New York speakers bureau, hasn't had much luck interesting big companies in its roster of specialists in the women's movement, it is doing big business on campuses and before women's groups.

Typically, feminist companies are more willing than conventional businesses to experiment with new, looser work patterns and organizational structures. Many are making a deliberate effort to break away from what they view as oppressive hierarchies existing in conventional companies. "The male is losing some of his human dignity" in traditional organizations, asserts Judith Meuli, who left a job as a technician at the University of California's Medical Center in Los Angeles to start selling jewelry, graphics and other feminist products. "The women I've talked to want to start their businesses . . . without losing some of their humanness," she says.

Anne Pride, a member of Know Inc., a Pittsburgh publishing concern, says, "We work as a collective and don't have any titles." In Washington, Carol Burris, a founder of Women's Lobby Inc., a firm formed to represent women's interests on Capitol Hill, says: "We're trying not to set up a male type of hierarchy where some women do all the interesting work and others do all the . . . work."

In practice, hang-loose work patterns tend to tighten up as a business expands and begins to confront thorny problems demanding the expertise of specialists. Know Inc. learned this lesson the hard way. After discovering that one member of the collective was engaged in old-fashioned embezzlement, it turned over its financial matters to a professional accounting firm.

1974   BILL HIERONYMUS

The New American Family

the things he cooks, everything from
d greens and cauliflower to peppers and
and tomatoes. Usually when he's done
ns up in the kitchen, too. I wouldn't
y other man or machine in the world."

extreme are those women who would
of the women's lib principles into prac-
id of how their husbands would react.
l assumes the militant women he sees
lesbians, that they don't have a man to
so they find other activities, like cru-
eir lives," says Arlene Canaday, a 26-
secretary. "My husband will take out
under severe duress and nagging, and
e grocery store once a month is a real
He's an artist and his studio is clut-
it himself because I'm not allowed in
he never helps around the house."

y says being a woman is a "drag." "I
ent our income, yet I'm also supposed
ve being domestic and look good doing
I? I'm tired when I come home. I'll
e I'm a secretary because I'm ashamed
yself. I feel that I should be more but

that women's-liberation activists are
nal is expressed by some women as well
n who was among several interviewed
e in New York snapped: "They're a
s, if you ask me. That's all I've got to
ne Bennington, 28-year-old wife of a
relations man, says: "I like being ca-
the other things that go along with
If they feel exploited, that's their prob-
ounch of frustrated biddies."

involvement of women from all walks

Let George Do It

R ICHARD Hansen finds it hard to iron his wife's
dresses. "There's so much material to cope with
that the sleeves never seem to come out looking right,"
he says.

But Mr. Hansen, a 23-year-old graduate student at
the University of Chicago, keeps trying. He has been
doing the ironing—and the cooking and cleaning as
well—ever since Kathleen, his wife of two years, convinced him that she was entitled to help around the
house so she could pursue a job as editor for a Chicago
publishing firm. "She's definitely not a homebody,"
says her husband. "She is very unhappy when she's
home doing housework."

In terms of the division of labor, at least, the Han-
sens' is scarcely a typical American marriage. But in
this age of increasingly vocal demands for "liberation"
on the part of women, it's not as unusual as you might
think.

More and more couples are pausing to reconsider
just what husbands and wives have a right to expect
from one another. Is there anything inherently "feminine," for instance, about the drudgery of housework—
or should husbands help with it to give wives more time
to pursue their own interests, particularly when they
also hold jobs outside the home? Or take the matter of
birth control: Is it entirely up to women or should men
assume more of the responsibility?

Many couples apparently have decided that at least some changes are in order. In interviews with scores of couples across the nation, Wall Street Journal reporters found many who had recently decided to alter a wide variety of living habits they had decided were unfair to the wife of the household.

Most changes, to be sure, seem trivial—and, indeed, to the more dedicated members of the women's liberation movement, they scarcely seem like changes at all. At best, most changes are just "tokenism—an appeasement," in the view of Roxey Bolton of Miami, financial vice president of the National Organization for Women, one of the oldest and largest feminist groups. "Now they want to get Mary out of the house a little more," says Mrs. Bolton.

In some cases, on the other hand, women's liberation leaders feel their movement is being perverted by women who use it to get special privileges for themselves. "Then all you have is a henpecked husband," says one New York woman active in the movement.

But for a sizable number of "Marys" who feel they have established new and better relationships with their husbands and, in the process, gained more personal freedom, it's an exhilarating experience.

Mrs. Albert Stern, a 42-year-old mother of three who lives in Cleveland, has made what she considers to be significant progress in changing some of the attitudes within her family since she joined a feminist discussion group six months ago. In the Stern household, she says, "there aren't any boy's jobs or girl's jobs anymore. Now the boys work in the kitchen. Once nobody could feed himself if I wasn't home to cook. That was my job. Now, if I'm not home, my husband cooks dinner himself."

Mr. Stern, a manufacturer's representative for storm window companies, has made other adjustments,

of life—including suburban, middle-class married women—makes it evident, however, that the presence or absence of husband and children can't be singled out as a motive. The many issues that fall under the feminist banner — ranging from demands that women be paid equally with men to the question of whether male "chivalry" is actually demeaning to women—include issues that appear to have strong appeal quite apart from a woman's own family circumstances.

The number of women's-liberation groups springing up in suburban areas is sizable. One particularly active chapter of the National Organization for Women in the New York area, for instance, is the group operating in Nassau and Suffolk counties on Long Island. The chapter, founded in 1969, "has been involved with all the well-publicized aspects of women's liberation," says its president, Rita Wroblewski. These include liberalized abortion laws, elimination of asserted sex discrimination in the public schools, the equal-pay issue and the establishment of child-care centers so mothers can work.

"The thrust for the coming year will be sex discrimination in education," Mrs. Wroblewski says. "At most junior high schools on Long Island, girls must take home economics and boys must take shop. We believe that it is wrong to have compulsory sex discrimination at that age—it immediately stereotypes some functions as male and others as female."

It's obvious, however, that some women find the liberation movement of interest mainly for its effect within their own homes. Some have become downright militant in insisting on an equitable distribution of household duties. A female newspaper reporter in Atlanta says she expects her husband to do precisely half the family laundry—or "he'll just have to go without underwear or socks."

A number of women feel particularly strongly on the issue of whether men should assume more responsibility for birth control—whether it should always be up to women to use the "pill" or some other method, or whether men should agree to sterilization in cases where a couple plans to have no more children.

Such proposals don't always get a warm reception from husbands. Carol Verblen, a public relations consultant in Chicago, is one who argues strongly that men should be willing to undergo vasectomies, or sterilization operations. "My husband thinks I'm crazy," she says. "He believes only women should be responsible. I've tried to persuade him over to my side, but he hasn't budged yet."

Plenty of husbands balk at other demands, too, whether they involve doing the shopping or washing dishes. But for some husbands who have agreed with their wives that changes would result in a more satisfactory relationship between them, the result has been rewarding.

James Stentzel of Nashville, managing editor of Motive, a United Methodist Church magazine, helps his wife, Cathrine, care for their 18-month-old son and does other household chores as a matter of routine. To him, such activities—and, indeed, the entire women's liberation movement—help "to make men more human" as well as benefiting women.

And Richard Hansen, the Chicago graduate student who irons his wife's dresses, finds more than just a practical meaning in his household labors. "Every week when I clean the house, I feel like I'm striking a blow for women's liberation," he says.

1970   —THE EDITORS

What Value Housework?

W HEN the insurance salesman called the other
night, the conversation went like this:

"Come right over," I said. "There is some coverage I
need. Disability insurance for my wife."

Pause. "Does she work?"

"Yes. She is a housewife."

Pause. "But is she a wage earner?"

"No."

Long pause. "I've been with my company 24 years.
I've never heard of disability coverage for housewives.
And besides, the company could take a tremendous
beating on this thing. What would prevent your wife
from filing a claim and then loafing around the house
all day? How would we know she was disabled?"

That one was easy. "The same way you'd check on
my disability," I replied. "And we need the coverage. Social Security will help support her if I am disabled while
the children are small. But if she is disabled, how can I
afford a housekeeper, cook, babysitter? When you find
out how to write that coverage, give me a call."

I'm still waiting.

It was nice, of course, to find an effective putdown
for an insurance salesman. But even that didn't make
up for my dismay at finding yet another example of society's jaundiced view of housework as a contribution to
society and as an expensive and difficult-to-replace ser-

vice. Housework doesn't even appear in Gross National Product figures unless a wife works and "hires" someone to perform the job.

There are signs, however, that the value to society of housework performed by women (and men) is slowly becoming recognized. The French government, for instance, reportedly is drafting a proposal for retirement pensions for all mothers. And in this country, the attitudes of both private insurers and the Social Security system are coming under increasing pressure.

The 1973 Joint Economic Committee hearings on economics problems of women touch on the housewife's economic dilemmas. In one hearing, for instance, Rep. Martha W. Griffiths asserted that complaints women are making against insurance companies document one of the "most serious forms of economic discrimination." In disability insurance, she said, women "are often forced to pay rates 50% to 100% higher than men for the same disability coverage." Yet statistics don't support such large differentials.

And Pennsylvania's Insurance Commissioner Herbert S. Denenberg noted that nonworking women often can't buy disability insurance at all. Women "should be able to buy disability insurance that fairly measures the economic value of childcare and homemaking," he asserted. "Traditionally, disability insurance has been sold only to income-producers on the theory that there must be an income to replace and an incentive to work. But a homemaker also makes a real economic contribution."

He acknowledged that insurers often assert they can't place a value on a homemaker's work. "But there have been plenty of court cases where a price was put on a homemaker's services," he said. "Occasionally, the woman turned out to be worth a lot more than her husband."

There are, of course, several ways to look at a housewife's "worth." A recent analysis by Changing Times Magazine suggests six. Most obvious is to break down the hours a housewife spends on various tasks and cost them out at the rate charged in the job market. Using this method, a Chase Manhattan Bank study found housewives working 99.6 hours a week at tasks which would cost $235.40 to purchase.

A simpler approach considers a housewife's job to be child care and housekeeping; Changing Times says five-day maid service commonly runs $80, day-care $40 a child, and baby-sitting $35 a week. If, however, a housewife is considered a home economist, professionals earn from $8,500 to $12,000 a year, the study notes.

For a woman who gives up a working career to be a housewife, her value might be viewed as the after-tax income she could earn if she wasn't working at home. Or, with both husband and wife essential to running a family, her time could be considered worth 50% of the family income.

Finally, as Mr. Denenberg notes, lawsuits occasionally set a value on a housewife's contribution. "The highest probable award to compensate for the accidental death of a full-time housewife would be about $35,000," Changing Times says, referring to court statistics.

The Social Security Administration, too, is under growing pressure to revise its view of housework. Women who don't "work" in the conventional sense are entitled to a number of benefits, of course, if their husbands are covered by the system. More than 13 million of the 23 million adults receiving Social Security payments in 1971 were women. Of the women, about half were receiving benefits based on their husbands' earnings records.

Nonetheless, a recent Social Security analysis notes, "Women are concerned that their work at home

—housekeeping activities and the care of children and of older family members who are ill or disabled—is not considered employment for Social Security purposes." Lack of coverage, moreover, means "there is no benefit to help meet the real cost of providing substitute homemaking and child care services in the event of the woman's death or severe disability."

Indeed, at present a family can't enroll a housewife in the Social Security system and pay the tax in order to secure the benefits, particularly disability payments, in event of her illness or death. (Mrs. Griffiths says she received a letter from an Oregon couple who planned to incorporate their farm and put the wife on the payroll in order to get Social Security coverage.)

To remedy that situation, Rep. Bella Abzug has introduced a bill that would establish a "householder's basic benefit" for a man or woman who maintains a household instead of working during the prime earning years. Such persons would be eligibile for benefits, financed out of general revenues, at the minimum levels paid "workers" enrolled in the system.

Two congressional witnesses proposed plans to give housewives Social Security credits. Carolyn Shaw Bell, professor of economics at Wellesley College, said society needs to change its view of women as being dependent. Noting that in Belgium an adult daughter up to 25 years old can receive a special payment if she stays at home as a housekeeper, she urged recognition in the Social Security system of "the non-paid work performed in the home," to be financed out of general revenues. And Wilbur J. Cohen, former U.S. Secretary of Health, Education and Welfare, asserted that women working at home should be eligible to contribute to the Social Security system at a rate similar to that paid by self-employed women.

Recognizing the "value" of housework would certainly have an impact on other aspects of the Social Security system. It likely would force a change in policies which can mean that a married woman who works outside the house may sometimes receive a retirement benefit no larger than that her husband's coverage would have earned for her anyway. It would pose a review of the present requirement that a divorced woman must have been married 20 years to receive a retirement benefit earned by her covered husband.

Moreover, Social Security credit for housework could give women who enter the work force later in life a base on which to build retirement payments. At present, the woman who begins working at age 40 or 50, and often at low paying jobs, has little chance for her Social Security contributions to qualify for a significant benefit.

And rethinking the housework question will affect men, too. A New Jersey man sued the Social Security Administration because regulations prevented him from receiving a "widow's" benefit.

Under Social Security, if a male covered wage earner dies, his young children receive monthly benefits and their mother receives a separate benefit until the children are grown. At present levels, such payments together for a widow and one child are worth about $6,000 a year.

In the New Jersey case, however, the wife was the covered worker through her job as a school teacher. Her husband did not have a full-time job. When she died in childbirth in 1972, he applied for the "widow's" benefit and was turned down. Asserting sex discrimination, he brought a lawsuit in federal court. His attorneys from the American Civil Liberties Union argued the policy makes a female wage earner's Social Security contributions worth less than a male's, and also discriminates against a male survivor. Society simply assumes "that men will never stay home with children," asserted attorney Ruth Bader Ginsburg. The "widow's" benefit, plus the dependent's benefit the child is already receiving, argued the father, would just about permit him financially to stay home and care for his infant son. [Late in 1973, the court ruled he was entitled to the benefits, retroactive to the time he first tried to apply.]

1973   —James C. Hyatt

The New Nomads

A NNE Adams is half apologetic about showing a visitor around her new suburban home in Middletown, N.J. Although it's a three-bedroom ranch house on a generous half acre of land, Mrs. Adams thinks it isn't nearly as nice as her former homes in Hartford, Conn., Lexington, Mass., Portsmouth, R.I., or Wellesley, Mass.

Since 1964, she has settled into five houses and two apartments, in six different cities. Although Brook Road in this suburban New Jersey development is her latest address, it won't be her last. For like many of her neighbors, she'll be moving on.

"Middletown is filled with people who say hello but don't bother to make friends because they know they won't be here long," the 34-year-old housewife says. "I'm the same way."

Some 40 million Americans move each year, and moving companies estimate corporate transfers propel over two and a half million of them. But Anne Adams belongs to a special group of these mobile Americans to whom moving is one of the few constants in their lives. They are wives of "executive nomads."

Although no van line charts their numbers, these women trail across the country following their husbands' careers. They go where the challenging job is, where the big opportunity opens up or where the next step in the corporate ladder leads. Some move with the energy that comes from being the push behind their corporate go-getter. Others, like Anne Adams, no less capable or supportive, move with the painful awareness of the personal costs of success.

"The price of success comes high," says Mrs. Adams with a rueful smile. "I always wanted to live on a tree-lined street in a small town where the kids could have the same friends and we the same neighbors for 20 years."

Instead, she hopscotched across the East following her husband's checkered career as variety store owner, Friendly Ice Cream Corp. trainee, salesman, country club manager, and since 1971, as an executive for McDonald's Corp. His last promotion, to field-and-labor-relations supervisor for McDonald's, landed him and his family in Middletown.

Such a transient life saps the strongest women and breaks the brittle. With each move, these executive wives are wrenched from friends, pulled from community involvement and often cut off from their own careers. Some become ignored casualties of success, dependent on alcohol, tranquilizers or barbiturates. Others simply run out of gas, depression experts say. These women are clinically depressed, lacking hope or desire, human sacrifices to upward mobility.

"Moving is a severe trauma probably as great as divorce," says Robert Seidenberg, a Syracuse, N.Y., psychiatrist, many of whose patients are victims of multimoves. "It's like uprooting a tree or a bush—you simply can't flourish transplanted five or six times."

Aside from the emotional trauma of moving, Dr. Seidenberg points out that the physical burden of moving is generally left to "the weaker sex." The wife packs, hires movers and often sells the house. While her husband forges ahead, she plods behind coordinating the movers with the children's school schedule. With the precision of a traffic controller, she times the family's departure one step ahead of the incoming owners and their arrival in their new home one step after the vacating sellers. Then, as her husband goes off to his new job, she's often left with the burden of unpacking and getting organized in the new place.

To ease the wife's work load, many companies work with such firms as Homerica or Metropolitan Relocation Center. Homerica, for example, will find the executive's wife another home, arrange selling her current one and brief the family on activities available in her new location. "We tell her where to go to make friends —the League of Women Voters, The Newcomers Club, or a political club," says Shirley de Lima, president of Homerica, whose corporate theme is "a happy wife is a happy transfer."

Still other companies are reevaluating their transfer policies. Many are eliminating needless lateral moves and are boosting incentives for transfers. "More and more, companies are becoming aware of the side-effects of relocation—the wife who becomes a recluse, the kids who all of a sudden become mavericks," says David North, president of David North & Associates, executive recruiters. "It affects their man and his performance."

While there is some effort to trim unnecessary transfers, most companies still shuffle their executives through the regional ranks before reeling them in to a top headquarters job. Wives of IBM officials joke, for instance, that the corporate initials stand for—"I've Been Moved."

For some families, picking up stakes again and again takes on an air of unreality. Keith Melville, a teacher of sociology at the City University of New York, recalls a wife of a friend who moved several times in the space of a few years. "She felt like it was a rerun of the

Lone Ranger," he says. "They were constantly riding out of one town or another with their newly found acquaintances waving good-bye and wondering who they really were."

No matter how practiced the family, each move still occasions fears and uncertainties. "You don't know what you're getting into, and when you have children you're afraid for them, too," says Mrs. Adams, mother of 3½-year-old Brooks Jr. and six-year-old Piage. "You don't want them to be lonely. You want them to meet friends, and you want the same things for yourself."

In the rush to get ahead, many husbands brush aside such fears. Most typically, they rush home and blurt out: "Honey, I've got great news—we're moving to Des Moines!" According to Dr. Seidenberg and others, the news carries a very different import for their wives.

In studies of depressed women at Yale University, for example, Myrna Weissman, project co-director of Yale's depression-research unit, observed that "while moving can be beneficial, it can also mean multiple losses to the individual—loss of important social ties, familiar living patterns, security. It is these losses that contribute to the development of depression."

Because mobility is an accepted part of American life, Mrs. Weissman feels its effects are vastly underrated and largely overlooked. In her clinical observations of depressed women, she discovered that often women didn't relate their illnesses to moving. More commonly, they attributed them to other events in their lives, such as financial problems, increased loneliness and identity confusion.

"In most cases, however, these other events were by-products of faulty adaptation to the stresses and changes created by moving," Mrs. Weissman says. In such instances, Homerica's hired hands don't help.

"The stress for the woman isn't the work, but the isolation and the loneliness," Mrs. Weissman says.

It's this stress that pulls at the Adams family. Eager to prove himself at his current job with McDonald's, Brooks Adams works long hours and is often away for a week at a time. In the lonely hours of such evenings, his pixie-haired wife watches television and works absently on a jigsaw puzzle. Anne Adams was at least prepared for this sort of life. The daughter of an electronics executive, Mrs. Adams is a child of a nomadic family. In pursuing his career, her father uprooted the family over 20 times. "I'm the only one of three sisters who spent all four years in one high school," she says.

After high school, she attended the University of Florida, where her father posed to her three career choices: nurse, secretary or teacher. She opted for the latter and, with a degree in education tucked in hand, headed for Boston to teach sixth grade.

There, the 25-year-old teacher met Brooks Adams, star high school halfback and a graduate of Boston University. He was then a 25-year-old owner of a university variety store—an enterprise that later fell victim to urban renewal. When they met, she little realized her life with the handsome store owner would bring a succession of moves. "I thought we'd be in Boston for the rest of our lives," she recalls.

As Mrs. Brooks Adams, she taught until their daughter Piage was born. Then, the transient life and child rearing veered her career to homemaker. For the time being, this means spending days and nights in the suburban quiet. "Do you know that song—'Is that all there is?'" she asks a visitor. "Well that's how I feel."

In Wellesley, she knew women who found solace in bridge parties, pills or liquor. But these aren't her answers. She is neither a joiner nor a heavy drinker.

"I can't stay at home and watch soap operas and eat bonbons," she confesses. "Probably I'll get a job so I can get out and talk to someone besides a six-year-old."

Although he is away a good deal of time, Brooks Adams realizes the strains on his wife and feels them, too. "There is nothing worse than picking up the phone when you're out of town, saying, 'Hello, how are you, I love you' and hearing a depressed person on the other end," he says.

For husbands, however, adjusting to a new community is easier. With each move they carry transferable career credentials and status. On the other hand, their wives start from scratch. In a new community where she knows no one, the executive nomad's wife is just another wife on the block with no identity of her own.

"In their old communities, the wives have been able to achieve some personal identity, in club or volunteer work, or they might have been known as good party givers," explains Dr. Seidenberg. "Then to renounce this maybe two or three times and start all over at the bottom—this is an inordinate kind of trauma most men couldn't take."

Dr. Seidenberg recalls one patient who had moved five times in seven years, following her husband's career as a chemist. When they came to Syracuse, the 27-year-old housewife got a real-estate job that she enjoyed and did well at. But her husband objected to her working weekends and forced her to give up her job. Four months later, she came to Dr. Seidenberg saying she had suicidal feelings. "Quitting her job was the last straw after all these other renunciations," Dr. Seidenberg says. "Typically, she thought she'd do violence. She didn't see the violence that had been done to her."

According to Dr. Seidenberg, each move brings greater personal and marital pressures. Often the accumulated strain becomes unbearable. Anne Adams remembers, for instance, one Friday night in 1973 when she met her husband for drinks and an early dinner. He had been out of town for a week, and when they met they had to get reacquainted. She told him what had happened to her during the week, and after three Scotch-and-waters she realized how inconsequential her concerns must seem to him. She began to cry, and all the pent-up loneliness and depression poured out. Finally, she recalls, she screamed: "I hate your job!—and I wish I had it!"

The strain of moving tumbleweed-like from one strange town to another often affects the children as well. The very young are apt to imagine the move as punishment for their behavior, doctors say. Like their mothers, children, too, have difficulty reestablishing their identities in a new community.

Both Brooks and Anne Adams worry about the effect their mobile life has on their children. Both children are shy, and their parents wonder if this is damage from multiple moves. "My daughter still wishes she lived back in Wellesley," worries Mrs. Adams, who is fairly certain that in a few years McDonald's will pull them from Middletown. "It shouldn't matter to a six-year-old where she lives."

Sometime in the future, when both children are in junior high school, Brooks Adams promises they'll settle down for good. Perhaps then they'll live on a tree-lined street in a small town where the kids play with the same friends, and they grow old with the same neighbors.

1973   —MARY BRALOVE

Doe vs. Doe

AT 9:30 one morning not long ago, Joan Frank walked into the Kings County Court House in Brooklyn, N.Y. to end a four-year marriage. At 3:15 p.m., 28 cases later, Mrs. Frank (not her real name) took the stand. The 24-year-old lab technician told the judge that her husband had left her when she became pregnant and refused to get an abortion. She also testified that her husband, on one occasion, had beaten her.

It was that last piece of information that nearly scotched Mrs. Frank's hopes for being granted a divorce. In Kings County, a spouse filing for divorce on the ground of "cruelty and inhuman treatment"—Mrs. Frank's chosen ground—must cite a minimum of two beatings. Joan Frank was aware of this stipulation; but, rather than compromise her integrity, she chose to tell the truth and hope for the best.

Mrs. Frank was fortunate. Although wrangling over legal technicalities dragged on that afternoon, the judge finally decided in her favor and granted the divorce. But her lawyer, despite the victory, has no kind words about divorce proceedings in Kings County. "It's a farce," the lawyer says. "People come in every day and make up stories, but in this case my client refused to lie."

The fact that anyone should have to lie to obtain a divorce—or, for that matter, should have to make any statement at all beyond an expression of intent—is currently being challenged by growing numbers of lawyers, disaffected spouses and others throughout the U.S. "There's a desperate need for divorce reform," says Dr. Gerald Gingrich, senior staff member of the Marriage Council of Philadelphia, which trains over a third of the nation's marriage counselors. "It's so disastrous for people to have to go through an adversary procedure to make possible new lifestyles for themselves."

Part of the pressure for divorce "reform" can be attributed to the sheer size of the community of the formerly married. According to the U.S. Bureau of the Census, in 1970, there were 15 million Americans who had been through a divorce. Preliminary estimates for 1971 indicate that 768,000 marriages ended in divorce that year, surpassing the prior record of 610,000 divorces in the postwar year of 1946.

But more than numbers is involved. According to observers, the increasing call for reform reflects a society in the throes of reshaping its values and relationships—a society in which growing numbers of men and women are pursuing romance but are frequently unwilling to cope with the often unromantic demands of marriage. "People want to get more out of life, and they're willing to put up with less and less," asserts Dr. Aaron Beck, a psychiatrist at the University of Pennsylvania.

Dr. Beck and others believe such an attitude is stemming from the women's liberation movement and the resulting changes in a wife's awareness of her role in a marriage. "Women are beginning to realize they don't have a white tornado coming in and doing the dishes. *They're* doing them," says Ann Garfinkle, a New York matrimonial lawyer. And when this thought process ends in the decision to get a divorce, both husbands and wives are increasingly unwilling to undergo the lengthy, and often humiliating, court proceedings usually required to obtain a divorce in the U.S. today.

In most states, for example, a spouse seeking a divorce must charge specific cruelties such as abandonment, adultery or mental abuse and often must rehash hurts long forgotten and best left buried. In many instances where a marriage simply died of boredom and mutual disinterest, divorce legalities tempt seekers to provide fictitious testimony.

To avoid such procedures, people are pressing state legislatures across the country to overhaul divorce laws. Women's-liberation groups, in particular, are pressing for state ratification of the Equal Rights Amendment to the Constitution, already passed by Congress, which would effectively end discriminatory grounds for divorce (such as charging a woman, but not a man, with desertion for not following a spouse to another state in the case of a business transfer). Other groups and individuals are advancing a variety of ideas: a one-year alimony limit; marriage contracts; divorce insurance; and "no fault" divorce, where both parties are held equally responsible for the marital breakdown.

Some of these ideas have already become law in certain states. California, for example, in 1970 passed a no-fault divorce bill whereby the court now will grant divorces based on "irreconcilable differences which have caused the irremediable breakdown of the marriage;" there needn't be an accuser and an accused. (The new law effectively eliminated all previous grounds for divorce in the state with the one exception of incurable insanity.)

Since California adopted its no-fault statute, other states have either replaced most of their previous grounds for divorce with no-fault provisions, or have added a no-fault plea to previously existing grounds. Nearly every state is currently weighing the use of no-fault in divorce cases. (New York and several other states already have a quasi-no-fault divorce system whereby a separation agreement may be automatically converted to a divorce after one year.)

Adoption of no-fault statutes, however, isn't being accomplished without heated debate, and the focal point for many opponents is the relative ease of obtaining no-fault divorce. "You shouldn't make it so easy that two people entering marriage can just walk in and say, 'We're through,'" says one no-fault foe, Eli Bronstein, a New York lawyer.

Some no-fault advocates charge that those no-fault opponents who are in the legal field are against the provision for fear of losing business. Most lawyers, however, say the situation is quite the contrary and that widespread adoption of no-fault would, in fact, bring about a business boost. "The bitterness will take place at the division of the spoils," one lawyer says. "There'll be more business than ever."

Certainly, dividing the spoils left in the wake of a wrecked marriage can be a trying business and often unfair to one party under numerous laws currently on the book. Take, for example, a case cited by Faith Seidenberg, a Syracuse lawyer. Mrs. Seidenberg's client, married seven years, had helped her husband day and night running a drugstore. Yet at the time of her divorce, the client was young enough to be employable, had no children to care for and therefore wasn't legally entitled to any money or property from her husband.

Mrs. Seidenberg's client isn't unusual, particularly in states like New York, where "community-property" statutes are lacking and assets at the time of divorce belong to the spouse in whose name the assets are recorded. According to women's-rights groups, court records are crammed with the histories of women who supported their husbands through law school, medical school or other graduate training and then, following divorce, ended up without a penny.

Faith Seidenberg and other lawyers argue that courts should award a wife compensation for past services rendered, whether those services may have been household chores or aid in operating a family business. A step in this direction, they say, would be the enactment of a community-property law like that of California or Texas; under such a statute, both spouses at the time of a divorce split the assets acquired during the marriage.

But critics charge that community-property laws can be inequitable, too. "If a woman has been a tramp, why reward her?" asks Mr. Bronstein, the New York lawyer. "By the same token, if a man is alley-catting around town, shouldn't his wife get all the benefits she had as a married woman?"

Such benefits are normally paid in the form of alimony (or "maintenance," as some prefer to call it—believing the term alimony has punitive overtones). But how is alimony to be determined? There apparently isn't any simple answer, and many courts have found that putting a price tag on certain chores attendant to a marriage is difficult indeed. Are cooking and caring for spouse and offspring labors of love or just plain hard labor? Some ex-husbands, while inclined to admit that a marriage involves genuine work on the wife's part, are nevertheless disinclined after divorce to pay their ex-wives alimony for unlimited amounts of time; but many ex-wives, citing a marital life of drudgery, want some sort of reimbursement for years of household work. (The argument, it should be noted, focuses on alimony, or a monetary award for the wife, rather than child support; few deny the husband's responsibility in sharing the support of his offspring.)

In an attempt to impose some order on this chaotic

situation, at least one group, the Committee for Fair Divorce and Alimony Laws, has sponsored bills to limit alimony payments to one year; longer payments would be left to judicial discretion, depending on a woman's age, employability and the age of the couple's children. Going one step further, the 200-member committee is also sponsoring bills in several states to abolish the "alimony jails" that many states maintain for men found delinquent in alimony or child-support payments. The committee considers such imprisonment a cruel and unusual punishment that should be barred under the Constitution.

According to some reformers, the fiscal and legal complexities of divorce could largely be eliminated if engaged couples, prior to the wedding day, were to contemplate the possibility of eventual estrangement. Along these lines, Lena K. Lee, a member of the Maryland legislature, has introduced a bill before that body calling for engaged couples to draw up a marriage contract, renewable at the option of either party three years from the date of the wedding; if irreconcilable differences are present at the end of the period, the contract isn't renewed, the marriage is legally terminated and accrued property is distributed according to contractual terms chosen by the couple.

"If I were buying a piece of property, I'd look at it from every angle," says the widowed Mrs. Lee. "A contract is trying to get people to be sensible about what they're doing and lay a foundation for a better life together."

Mrs. Lee's fellow legislators defeated her proposal, but she says she has no plans to give up the fight. On another front, The National Organization to Insure Support Enforcement (N.O.I.S.E.) is proposing the idea of divorce insurance to be taken out by young marrieds against the possibility of financial hardships ensuing from a future divorce.

According to N.O.I.S.E., to be actuarially feasible, divorce insurance would be made available to couples married at least five years and could eventually be converted to additional life insurance, retirement benefits or educational funds if the couple ends up staying together. Thus far, no such plan exists; but Diana Du-Broff, founder and president of N.O.I.S.E., believes the insurance would serve a very real need.

"The money would allow the dependent spouse to become a wage earner and help maintain the family after the first shock of divorce," Mrs. DuBroff says. "A parent couldn't find a better wedding gift."

1973   —MARY BRALOVE

Breaking Up

TO all appearances, it was a typical middle-class marriage, thriving and stable in suburbia.

"I had an accountant husband, three kids, two cars, a nice home—the whole works," recalls Joan. "I never gave it much thought, but I assumed I was happy. At least I never felt especially unhappy."

Then, she says, one day "I discovered that I couldn't stand the man I was living with and probably never could."

So in 1969, Joan (not her real name), a pretty, intense dark-haired woman of 32, got a divorce from Philip (also not his real name), her husband of 10 years. She still lives with her children in the seven-room, red-brick ranch house that she and Philip bought for $30,-000 in the third year of their marriage, but instead of housewifely chores she now works as an executive secretary in a large Chicago firm while a housekeeper takes care of the kids.

Joan says she is "much, much" happier now than she was when she was married, but she admits that her adjustment to divorced life—an adjustment that is still in process—hasn't been smooth or easy. "When you get right down to it, you realize that nothing is the same as it used to be," she says. "I've gotten rid of one set of problems, but I've picked up another."

In doing so, Joan is far from alone. According to the Census Bureau, in 1970, 15 million Americans had been through a marriage breakup at one time or another and more than four million Americans listed their marital status as divorced. Some 60% of them were women. The ratio is lopsided partly because women tend to outlive their ex-husbands and partly because the chances of remarriage are better for a divorced man than a woman.

The divorced population of the U.S. has swollen rapidly in recent years. In 1969, an estimated 660,000 marriages ended in divorce in this country, 13% more than in 1968 and the highest one-year total ever. Based on population, the 1969 divorce rate wasn't quite as high as it was in 1946 when 610,000 marriages, many of them hasty wartime unions, came apart. "That (postwar) period was clearly an abnormal one," says a U.S. Census Bureau official. "What we are seeing now is a steady uptrend that appears bound to continue."

Social scientists attribute the growing procession of Americans to the divorce courts to a number of factors. They say that the increasingly mobile nature of American life has contributed to divorce by reducing family stability. The improved economic status of women—coupled with the recent general affluence—has made divorce a more feasible alternative to unhappy wives. Indeed, authorities say, these developments and others have combined to change marriage from the predominantly economic institution of the past century to one that is based—and judged—primarily on its ability to satisfy the emotional needs of the persons involved.

The divorce process itself has become easier as state after state has relaxed its legal requirements. Changing social mores have lessened, though not removed, the stigma that used to attach to divorce. The adjustment of divorced persons to "single" life has been smoothed further by the widespread advent of clubs of formerly married persons formed specifically for that purpose.

All that notwithstanding, divorce almost invariably has a deep and disturbing effect on the lives of the people who undertake it. For both men and women, the immediate post-separation period frequently is marked by physical and psychological ills, some of which go away. Except for the wealthy, a marriage split almost always makes both parties worse off financially than they were before. Old friends are lost, so new ones must be made. Relationships with children change, usually for the worse.

For the divorced woman, there are often additional problems. "Unlike most men, most women have never really been on their own until their divorce," says thrice-married Mrs. Louise Athern of San Francisco, who as Louise Rohner wrote the best-selling book "The Divorcee's Handbook." She adds: "Even the worst marriage gives a woman some security. When she divorces, it's a shock to realize that if things are going to get done, she, and no one else, is going to have to do them."

On top of that, many divorcees find themselves "out of position" to accomplish the things they want, says Dr. Dean Ackley, a psychiatrist affiliated with the Los Angeles domestic relations court. "If the divorced woman with children wants a career, she has to cope with the fact that she won't be able to give her kids the attention they may need," he explains. "If she wants to remarry, she quickly finds out that she has plenty of competition from women who can present men with fewer problems than she does."

Joan has encountered all of those difficulties to one degree or another since she and Philip separated in 1968. And while her secretarial salary plus the child support money she receives from Phil puts her income well above average, she has much in common with many other divorcees.

Indeed, many of the same things that made Joan

and Phil like many married couples their age also make them a fairly typical divorced pair. Like more than 60% of all marriages that break up, theirs involved children under 18 years of age. The duration of their marriage was just a few years more than the median of 7.1 years for all U.S. marriages that end in divorce. (Almost 40% of the marriages that break up survive 10 years or more.)

Lawyers say that the idea of an amicable, or friendly, divorce is largely a myth. "If a couple is amicable, they stay married," says Robert Veit Sherwin, a New York divorce attorney and author. Joan's and Phil's divorce is no exception. In the year following their divorce, they went to court four times, three times over money (Joan wanted and eventually got a larger monthly sum for child support) and once when she obtained an injunction barring Phil from the house after he pushed her down during an argument that erupted on one of his visits to the children.

Nor has living apart dulled the bitterness between Joan and Phil. "She's a hostile little bitch. She hasn't missed a chance to make it tough for me," says Phil.

Says Joan: "He's still a mediocrity and he always will be. All I feel for him is pity."

Joan thinks that, in retrospect, her marriage was a mistake from the beginning. Authorities in the field say this reaction is typical and usually true. "My psychologist told me that a lot of people put more planning into a trip to the movies than they put into picking the person they'll marry," Joan says. "I guess that was the way it was with me."

The couple met on a blind date. Philip, four years older than Joan, was a practicing accountant at the time; Joan was a secretary who had dropped out of college after two years. A good student in high school, she says she found college work "just too hard." The months after she left college were difficult ones for Joan. Dropping out of college "really took me down," she says. Most of her girl friends either were married or preparing to get married. "It made me feel like a failure," she says.

"That's when Phil came along," she continues. "I didn't really like him at first, but he was persistent. I was impressed that he was an older man with a profession, and he struck me as being mature because things didn't seem to bother him the way they did me. When he asked me to marry him, I said yes. I'd made up my mind I was done looking."

The couple's married life quickly settled into routine. Joan continued to work during the early years of the marriage, quitting shortly before their first child, Melissa, now eight, was born. At about that time, she and Phil made a down payment of $8,000—most of which Phil had saved before the marriage—and bought the home that Joan now occupies. In the next four years two more children were born: Bryan, now six, and Peter, now four.

Joan says she never liked housework but still "went all out" to be a good housewife. She couldn't cook well before she married, so she attempted to remedy that (successfully, says Phil) by going to cooking school. In addition, "my house was always immaculate," she says. "I made a science out of things like scrubbing floors; I timed myself to see how I could do it most efficiently. If Phil had smoked, I would have lurked around him wiping up his ashtray. That was the kind of housekeeper I was."

The couple pursued a normal suburban social life. They took up bridge and became involved—although casually—in various religious and civic groups. Phil changed employers several times in the early years of the marriage but then took a partner and opened his own small accounting firm. His income climbed slowly but steadily.

This period of seeming tranquility lasted about eight years, but Joan says that problems were building from the first. "We argued over money," she says. "Phil was very cheap and hated to see me spend, but once in a while I'd go out and really splurge. I'd buy a couple hundred dollars worth of clothes for the kids, or four or five pairs of shoes at a time for me. I knew he wouldn't like it, but I did it anyway. I suppose I felt I had to. I knew I would win any argument we'd get into over it."

The couple's sex life "always was bad," Joan says. "I was a virgin when I got married. When Phil and I didn't hit it off sexually, I figured that was just the way it was. I didn't like it and tried to get out of it whenever I could. I never told Phil this right out—that would have been too honest—but I made up the usual excuses. He complained at first, but then he gave up. For all purposes, we had no sex life."

Otherwise, she says, "we each had our own little shells. After dinner, he would work or read. I'd sew or watch TV. There was no communication between us. I don't think we had a serious discussion in all the years we were married."

What brought these problems to a head was Joan's decision to lose weight shortly after her third child was born. Joan is five-feet-one and had been overweight since childhood. She weighed a chubby 120 pounds when she was married, and eight years of married life had increased this to 140 pounds. "Phil, my mother, everybody was nagging me to lose weight, so I gave in," she says.

Joan joined an organization of women trying to shed pounds—"a sort of fat ladies' anonymous," she says—and stuck with its program. In four months she lost 35 pounds. It changed more than her figure. "It did something for my whole outlook," she says with a trace of wonder. "I looked good and I felt good. Everybody told me how great I looked. I'd never thought of myself as a desirable woman—that's probably why I married Phil in the first place—but suddenly I did. I felt I had to go out and be with people to show them how great I was."

The new, slim Joan stepped up her organization work, spending less and less time at home. At one group she met "a wonderful, witty older man, someone I could really talk to." She goes on: "We talked about politics, religion, everything. Some people started to kid us about having a 'thing' together, but it was never anything like that. He made me think about who I was and what I was doing, which was something I'd never done before.

"Once I was complaining to him about how I had to be in charge of a lunch for a women's club I belonged to. He asked me why I *had* to do it. I thought it over, and I couldn't come up with a reason. The next day I called the thing off. I'd discovered I could change things just by saying no."

That discovery, she says, "liberated me." It also upset her. She began having headaches, feeling tense and finding it hard to sleep. "I went to a doctor, and he examined me. He said, 'Okay, there's nothing wrong with you, so what's wrong?' Before I knew it, I was blurting out that I hated my husband. It came out, just like that, but I knew it was true. I went home and told Phil I wanted a divorce."

It wasn't that simple, of course. Philip, taken by surprise, resisted the move. At his insistence, the couple consulted two different marriage counselors, but to no avail; Joan says her mind was made up. Several heated arguments took place in the next few weeks, during which Joan "threw a few dishes" to make her point. Finally, one Saturday, "he got a U-haul trailer and moved his stuff out," she says.

The days immediately after Philip left "were the happiest of my life," says Joan. "I took the kids and we stayed with my mother that first night, then we came back home the next day. When I walked into that empty house, I had the most wonderful feeling of independence. There was no one to nag or criticize me. I felt free."

This feeling lasted about a month. Then, typically, complications set in. "When the newness wore off, I didn't know how to handle being alone," she says. "I started feeling very guilty and remorseful. Little things the children did started to bother me. I'd start crying for no reason. All of a sudden, everything came loose." She says that "to understand what had happened to me," she began visits to a psychologist that were to continue for a year and a half.

At the same time, Joan had to come to grips with the complex financial and custodial negotiations that accompany separation and divorce. Lawyers say that this is often the most difficult period for divorcees and that under emotional stress they sometimes make hasty, conciliatory decisions that they later live to regret. According to Joan, however, she avoided this pitfall.

"Upset as I was, I had the sense to call a good divorce lawyer and put myself in his hands right after Phil left," she says. "I'd seen other women get soft about things in their divorces and come out badly, and I didn't want that to happen to me. It just meant too damned much to me and the kids."

On her lawyer's advice, Joan didn't go to work until about nine months after Philip left, even though she had to borrow money from her mother to make ends meet because the $450 a month that Philip had agreed to pay her in temporary support didn't cover her bills. "The lawyer thought I'd get a bigger settlement if I didn't work," she explains.

Also on her attorney's advice, Joan didn't go out with men for the one-year period between her separation and divorce, although she did belong to several clubs that included men. "There were plenty of times I wanted to go out, especially after Phil started dating, but my lawyer put his foot down," she says. "He said that dating was the worst thing I could do. He said it would make Phil mad, and that would lead to trouble in the negotiations."

Those tactics worked and Joan obtained what she calls a "very good" settlement. Phil agreed not to contest the divorce action, and she received a decree on the ground of "mental cruelty." In addition to custody of the children, she got to keep the house, its furnishings and one of the two cars. Phil agreed to pay $400 a month in child support, plus any "extraordinary" medical expenses incurred by the children. Six months later, over Phil's objections, Joan won an increase in her monthly cash allowance to $435 on the ground that Phil's income had climbed to $17,000 a year, or about $1,400 a month, from the $14,500 a year, or about $1,200 a month, upon which the first settlement was based. (Should Phil's income increase again, Joan may again ask the court for more money.)

But the main bone of contention was the house. Phil wanted to sell it to get his half of the $18,000 equity. "That represented about all the wealth I had," he says. Joan resisted. "Selling the house would have meant uprooting the kids and forcing them to change schools," she says. "They'd been through enough without that." In the end, Phil agreed to let Joan stay put; in turn, he will get his $9,000 if she sells the house or remarries and remains in it.

The $5,220 a year Phil pays Joan is about 30% of his annual income. Judges usually award wives with children from 33% to 50% of their ex-husbands' gross earnings. Still, Joan comes out well ahead of most divorced women, simply because Phil earns far more than the U.S. median family income of $8,500. Even so, she says, $435 a month isn't nearly enough to live on, so she relies on her own earnings for most of her income.

Those earnings are healthy; unlike many divorcees, Joan has a skill. As a secretary to two top executives of a manufacturing firm, her base pay is $140 a week and she regularly boosts that by putting in overtime. In 1969 she earned $8,800. With the $5,200 in child support, it puts her income at over $13,000, more than the $12,000 Phil has left after he pays the child support.

Joan says that kind of money is more than enough for her needs, even after the $60 a week she pays her live-in housekeeper. In the year following the divorce, she bought a new car, put $450 into a mutual fund and repaid much of the $1,350 borrowed from her mother during her separation.

Joan feels "a little guilty" because all that overtime keeps her away from the children; sometimes they're in bed when she gets home. But she keeps at it, and not for the money alone. "I get a feeling of accomplishment from my job that I never got when I was home," she says. "And I'm crazy about my bosses because they are such competent men. I enjoy being around competent men."

Establishing a social life after 10 years of marriage was much harder than going back to work. At first, some of Joan's married female friends went out of their way to be friendly after her separation. ("Immediately after a split, the woman usually gets treated as though her husband had died," says Max Marcus, a Chicago social worker who counsels many divorced persons.) But

Joan soon found she had little in common with such friends and drifted away. She says aside from a few friends she has known from childhood, most of her present women friends are other divorcees. "We just seem to gravitate together."

Meeting men posed another problem. Joan says she "really didn't know how to get started there" and had "a few false starts." Once, a divorced girl friend "dragged" her to a "singles" bar, but she didn't like it. "It seemed to be full of married men looking for action," she says. "That decidedly wasn't for me."

Nor were several dances and meetings given by clubs for formerly married persons. Joan attended a few but failed to meet a man she liked. Joining a bridge club —she was steered to it by another divorced girl friend —was more successful. The atmosphere "wasn't as strained as at places where people just go to meet other people," she says, "and I liked it a lot." She met "all kinds of new people—married, single and divorced," including the two men she has dated most, one a bachelor, the other a divorced man. The club is also where she goes for "adult companionship, meeting men aside."

Finding a possible marriage partner is more difficult. Joan says she likes the man she's now dating, a bachelor one year younger than she, but she doesn't think he's ready "to face marriage" yet. Among other things, "his parents don't like him seeing me. They're the kind of people who think that once someone is married they should stay married, no matter what. To say that they don't approve of me is an understatement."

As for the divorced men she has dated, "they're too broke from paying off their ex-wives to think about marrying again right away," she says. "I'm discovering that most of the nice men around are happily married, and that most of what's left are fellows with problems.

If that wasn't enough, not every man wants a ready-made family with three kids," she adds.

Nonetheless, Joan says, her relationships with men are a distinct improvement over the past. She has had sex with several men since her divorce, and she says she is enjoying it for the first time. "I'm a big girl now, so I can't see any reason why I shouldn't go to bed with men I like, as long as I'm discreet about it," she says.

Joan says her children "have been just great" since the divorce; "they've hardly batted an eyelash through the whole thing." But then she adds: "Melissa (the eight-year-old) has been staying up until 11 or 11:30 at night. I'm not too worried about that, though, because she gets up fine every morning. I guess she doesn't need that much sleep."

Bryan, the six-year-old, had "some trouble with his reading" after the divorce and now receives psychological counseling at school. Phil pays the $12 weekly charge for that. Bryan's reading has improved, but the psychologist believes the sessions should continue for a while.

Peter, the youngest, was only two when his parents separated—"too young to know what was going on," says Joan. "He didn't sleep well for a few nights after Phil left—he said he saw spiders in his bed—but that went away and he's been doing all right since."

Phil visits the children between noon and 5:30 p.m. on Sundays and on Thursday evenings from six to nine. Except for the shoving incident that led Joan to get a court order barring him from the house ("I don't know what got into him," she says), the visits have gone smoothly. "As long as he doesn't come into the house, he can see the kids as often as he wants. I asked for the divorce, so who am I to keep him from his children? It makes me angry when I hear about other divorced women giving their ex-husbands a hard time about that."

Joan says the children "seem to like Phil all right, even if he never had much time for them when he was still with me. Sometimes they're a little crabby after his visits, but they don't moon for him."

All in all, Joan says, "things have turned out fine for me." She would like to remarry someday but says she's in no hurry. "One thing for sure is that if I do remarry I'll never sit in a house all day again," she says.

1970   —FREDERICK C. KLEIN

Explaining the Baby Bust

IT'S unsettling to contemplate, but America's future is being decidedly altered by decisions being made today—in the nation's bedrooms.

Millions of us, for reasons that aren't clear, have decided to bring fewer children into the world than did our parents—a collective decision that makes zero population growth a distinct possibility. Under the right conditions, some demographers predict, it's even possible there may be a *decline* in population early in the next century.

While the experts still don't fully comprehend previous great shifts in national fertility there are nevertheless many explanations offered for the current baby bust. They include a social awareness that unchecked population growth may outstrip natural resources, the availability of effective contraceptives, and easier access to abortion. Overlying all these possible reasons, and possibly the major factor, are concerns about the economy, about inflation, about living the lifestyle we'd like to and how many children, if any, fit into that picture.

Putting motivations aside for the moment, let's consider what our collective bedroom decisions have thus far accomplished.

Anyone who has paid school taxes during the 1950s and 1960s has paid the price of the unprecedented baby boom that followed World War II. The boom peaked in

1957 with a whopping 4.3 million births. Now the children born during that population explosion are entering their reproductive years—a veritable launching pad for yet another cycle of booming diaper services, baby food sales and crowded schools.

Since the 1957 birth peak, the birth rate has gradually declined. But when the decline reversed in 1969 and increased again the next year, demographers naturally assumed it was the beginning of a new boom to be produced by the daughters of the postwar baby crop coming of age.

But in 1971, the birth rate resumed its post-1957 decline, at an even steeper rate than before, ending up 4% below 1970. You could almost hear the brakes screeching in 1972 as the birth rate dropped another 8.4%.

In 1973, fertility continued to drop. Despite the fact that the U.S. currently has the largest number of potential mothers in its history, there were fewer than 3.2 million babies born that year, the lowest number for any year since 1945. The birth rate—the number of babies born for each 1,000 population—dipped to 15, the lowest in U.S. history. Even at the depths of the Depression the birth rate hadn't gone below 18.

In October 1973, the fertility rate—the number of babies born to each 1,000 women between the ages of 15 and 44, the prime reproductive years—dropped to 66.6, also a new low. It was 123 in 1957.

The total number of babies born in 1973 was so low that, if continued, total population would drop. For the first time we dropped below the so-called replacement level—the number of children statistically required to replace their parents. (Each couple must produce 2.1 children, to allow for deaths. In 1973, we reproduced at a 1.9 rate.)

Statistics, however, don't take motivations into account, and last year's fertility measurements may be spurious. A more meaningful measure would be completed fertility. Today's couples are having children later in marriage, but who is to say they won't end up with total family sizes well above the replacement level?

Indeed, it's estimated that more than half of the upward and downward shifts in fertility over the years can be explained by shifts in the average age at which women have their children. A shift to births earlier in marriage would make a baby boom more pronounced, while a baby bust such as today's is accentuated by a trend toward delayed family building.

Even if families were to continue reproducing at a level below that required for replacement, it would be decades before total population actually began to shrink, given the relatively larger size of that segment of the population which is doing the reproducing.

Is the zero population growth level we reached last year only an aberration, to be swallowed up by "catch-up" pregnancies? Or is it a long-term trend?

Norman B. Ryder, representing a majority view among demographers, thinks it's more realistic to assume that couples now in the mainstream of raising families will end up with a total number of children exceeding the replacement level by 10% or more. But Prof. Ryder, co-director of the government-sponsored National Fertility Project, at Princeton University, adds, "it's quite plausible to speculate that we're approaching an era of declining population." Assuming a fertility pattern not too different from today, he sees U.S. population growing from its present 210 million to about 270 million in the next 50 years, and then going into decline.

Paul H. Jacobson, a population expert at Metropolitan Life Insurance Co. in New York, calculates that more than 1.2 million births were "postponed" between 1971 and 1974. Barring unforeseen economic catastrophe or war, he estimates, 85% of those postponed babies will be "made up" by 1979. Mr. Jacobson predicts that by 1975 total annual births will exceed the record of 4.3 million set in 1957 and exceed 4.5 million annually from 1978 through 1980.

Mr. Jacobson doesn't see any change, however, in the decades-old trend toward smaller family size, nor does he see zero population growth anywhere near. "Two or three children will continue to be a popular family size," he says, meaning that families will be reproducing at above the 2.1 replacement rate.

The most recent annual survey of anticipated family size, conducted by the Bureau of the Census in 1973, bears out Mr. Jacobson's contention. It shows that almost 70% of married women intend to have between two and three children. To drop below the replacement level, Americans would have to break the "two-child-barrier," which doesn't appear in the cards. The Census Bureau, however, does report a continued increase in the number of women who expect to have only one child or none, and a continued decrease in the number of women who expect four or more children. Both groups remain small in proportion to the mainstream, however.

Larry L. Bumpass, of the Center for Demography and Ecology at the University of Wisconsin at Madison, on the other hand, thinks the Census Bureau figures overstate eventual family sizes.

Writing in Family Planning Perspectives, Prof. Bumpass predicts that the current decline in fertility hasn't yet reached bottom and says fertility "is likely to hover below replacement—perhaps rather far below."

While he admits that recent low birth rates may indeed simply be a matter of delayed marriages and births, Prof. Bumpass believes they reflect instead a "revolution in the fertility regime."

Today's birth-control methods, unlike those of the

past, offer almost complete protection from pregnancy, he points out. Previously, when no woman could confidently plan on a lifetime of childlessness, he says, "the adult role expectations of women were structured around motherhood (as) rationalizations of the inevitable."

The young women of today, with ready access to and increasing knowledge of the birth-control pill, intra-uterine devices, sterilization and abortion, can be expected to ascribe less often to motherhood as their only alternative, Prof. Bumpass speculates. More young women are "finding increasing gratification in their jobs and freedom from the intensive demands of infant child-care," he says. Aggregate fertility goals, as expressed in the Census Bureau studies, may never be reached, "perhaps with many women remaining childless," he says.

To be sure, the availability of better contraceptives doesn't insure that they will be used. Few would argue that the reason women are having fewer children is due alone to better contraception. There has to be a difference in motivation between today's couples and those of previous generations. In past periods of economic downturn, for example, Americans reduced their fertility *without* effective contraception, apparently mostly by sheer willpower.

Richard A. Easterlin, professor of economics at the University of Pennsylvania, contends that the fertility of young adults corresponds closely to their relative affluence, that is, how affluent they are compared to how well off they'd like to be. The baby boom after the war, he says, can be explained by the fact that young adults were able to achieve income quite high in relation to their expectations. In recent years, Prof. Easterlin notes, the relatively larger number of young adults entering the marketplace have found it increasingly difficult to meet their economic goals.

"Young people today are really under more economic stress than their counterparts in the '50s and '60s," he says, and should have small families as a result. It also follows that because today's families will be smaller, the children of those families who reach adulthood in the next decades may face less competition, do better economically, and enjoy higher fertility as a result.

Alternately, while the birth rate has dropped in the past without the availability of effective birth control methods, there's little doubt that their availability today is accentuating the fertility decline.

In 1971, for example, while the national fertility rate dropped 6% from the year before, it dropped twice as much in New York State and California following reform of abortion laws in those two states which made abortion easy to obtain. Connecticut, whose residents have convenient access to New York's abortion clinics, recorded a 22% drop in births in 1972.

Sterilization procedures, both for men and women, are becoming increasingly popular. It's estimated that by 1970, as many as one of every six couples who had the children they wanted had been sterilized. The procedure greatly shortens the time span during which a couple would normally be "at risk" of having an unwanted pregnancy.

In summary, it's difficult to accept the argument made by some zero growth advocates that many couples are limiting their family size because of concern about possible world overpopulation. Great social issues usually have little impact at that level. Instead, personal economic concerns appear to be the most crucial of the many intricately intertwined factors contributing to the birth rate slide. In past periods of economic pressure, the drop in the birth rate was limited by the lack of effective means of birth control. With the mastery of these birth control methods by the majority of Americans, giving them the power to turn on and off their fertility at will, we can expect sharp, roller-coaster changes in fertility in the future, in lockstep with changes in perceived prosperity.

1974   —BARRY KRAMER

Campus Revolt

Bias In Academia

MARGARET Cussler, an associate professor of sociology at the University of Maryland, is paid $2,-000 less than anyone else at her level in her department, but she claims that's just one of her worries.

Prof. Cussler, who has taught at the university since 1954, says her department has blocked her advancement by refusing to help her get research grants, by not assigning her to teach "important" courses and by denying her key faculty committee appointments. In December 1970, the four men in her department who outrank her turned down her request to become a full professor with tenure.

"If I were a man, there would be no question about my promotion or anything else," she asserts. "My credentials are better than those of the men who turned me down."

But wait. Can there be sexual bias in academia, that supposed bastion of tolerance and reasonableness? You'd better believe it, claim women faculty members at colleges and universities across the country. Many of them are organizing local campus pressure groups and filing complaints against their employers with the federal government under a 1968 presidential order barring sex discrimination by federal contractors. Under attack are university hiring and promotion procedures and salary levels for women.

143

Many male academicians argue that the women—including Prof. Cussler—are exaggerating the problem. "Like other complaints in this category, Prof. Cussler's case isn't black and white," contends her department chairman, Prof. Robert A. Ellis. Indeed, a university committee to which Prof. Cussler took her gripes recommended a salary increase but found no grounds for charges of discrimination in promotion procedures.

Nationwide, however, there is statistical evidence that women don't advance at the same rate as men, for whatever reason. According to the U.S. Office of Education, women account for about one-fifth of the nation's 533,000 faculty members. Recent surveys show that 35% of faculty women hold the rank of instructor, the lowest in academia, while only 9% are full professors; among faculty males, 16% are instructors and 25% are full professors.

Salaries for women college teachers are lower across the board than those of their male colleagues. The American Council on Education, a private research group, reports that in 1969, 63% of faculty women were paid less than $10,000 a year while only 28% of faculty men earned less than that amount.

Moreover, faculty women tend to be clustered in such traditionally female fields as home economics, education, nursing and the social services—while men dominate the more prestigious liberal arts and sciences. At the University of Wisconsin's College of Letters and Sciences in 1970, 25 of the 55 departments had no women members, while only 19 of the 561 tenured professors in the college were women. Women made up just 2% of the full professors at the University of California at Berkeley in 1971. Harvard University, in a report on the status of women on its staffs, stated that "women had been virtually absent" from the upper ranks of its arts and sciences departments.

In some respects, academic women actually have lost ground of late. Since the mid-1960s, men have replaced women as presidents of prestigious Sarah Lawrence, Bryn Mawr and Vassar colleges. Overall, women accounted for 28% of all college teachers in 1930 compared to 20% in 1971, the Office of Education says.

Many university officials say that these comparisons aren't necessarily the result of discrimination. Mainly they base their reluctance to hire women for faculty posts on the belief that women will quickly quit to marry and raise families.

For a woman who wants to work, a husband or child can be a liability, says Lane Davis, a professor of political science at the University of Iowa. "We tried to hire one woman but she wanted us to hire her husband, too. Now what in hell were we going to do with him?" he asks. Pregnancies present special problems, particularly if a woman who is a department's only specialist leaves for a year, officials say.

"On the whole, women aren't able to make the reputation as scholars that men are," says Richard Lester, dean of faculty at Princeton University. "Family responsibilities make it hard for them to keep up to date in their fields and to turn out as much research as men do."

That may be true in some cases, critics concede, but they claim that the small number of women in many areas of acadamia stems directly from bias in hiring and promoting. Women critics say some men feel that a large number of women in a field will lower its prestige. "I have men on the staff who will vote against a woman for a job just because she's a woman. They just don't want women around," says one Harvard department head.

Moreover, whether intentionally or not, traditional academic hiring practices tend to work against women when it comes to filling prestigious posts, say campus women's groups. Top-flight colleges typically don't advertise openings, and often it's considered bad form to apply for a job; professors wait to be called. When a department has an opening, its ranking members commonly contact their colleagues at other institutions to ask for recommendations and then invite one or two favored candidates to visit the campus.

Women have dubbed this the "old buddy system." Shirley Clark, associate professor of sociology and education at the University of Minnesota, says: "It may not be as blatant as an application returned to you stamped 'male only,' but it works the same way. A woman is at a disadvantage once a department chairman so much as uses masculine pronouns to describe the person he wants to hire."

Another obstacle to women in academia has been rules that forbid both husband and wife from working in the same institution or in the same department. The rules, designed to prevent such problems as one spouse passing judgment on another, don't discriminate on the basis of sex. But when, as frequently happens, an academic woman marries an academic man, it's usually her career that's sacrificed.

Consider the case of Margaret Harlow, who was an assistant professor of psychology at the University of Wisconsin when she married another professor in the department in 1948. Faced with a university rule against nepotism, she resigned her post. She spent most of the next 17 years assisting her husband and his colleagues in their research without formal recognition or pay.

In 1965, the university bent its regulations enough to allow Prof. Harlow to be a lecturer in another department. But it wasn't until 1970—22 years after she was forced to resign—that the university finally agreed to make her a full professor. "I could cry when I think of all the years I lost because of that silly rule," she says.

Academic women have made some headway in removing barriers to their progress, however. Nepotism rules have been revised at the universities of Arizona, Michigan, Pittsburgh and Wisconsin. Tufts University has established a university-wide clearing house for hiring that not only publicizes faculty vacancies but seeks out and encourages women and minority-group candidates to apply.

Individuals and groups have filed more than 250 employment discrimination complaints against colleges with the federal government under the 1968 antibias order. But widespread results aren't expected to come soon because the Department of Health, Education and Welfare, which is charged with enforcing the rule, has only a small investigation staff.

However, one complaint led to the withholding of some $7.5 million in federal contracts from the University of Michigan until it came up with an acceptable plan to end sex discrimination. Among other things, Michigan agreed to give women staffers an estimated total of about $6 million in back pay, retroactive to 1968, to make up for past salary inequities. Contracts totaling about $3 million also were withheld from Harvard University until it furnished previously unreleased information about its hiring practices.

1971   —SUSAN B. MILLER

Two for the Price of One

STEVE Brenner and his wife, Pat, began searching for jobs teaching college economics in early 1973. After scores of interviews and rejections, they each finally got an offer: from two colleges separated by 50 miles of winding mountain road. If both were to accept, "it would have meant living apart during the week," Pat says.

A decade or so ago, if a young couple was faced with that prospect, the husband typically would have accepted his job offer, while the wife put her career in abeyance and dutifully followed him. But because the Brenners, like many couples, believe both husband and wife should be free to pursue careers, they settled on an intriguing alternative: sharing one job. Together, they accepted a $12,450 teaching position at Grinnell College, a small, liberal-arts school in Grinnell, Iowa.

Like three other job-sharing couples at Grinnell, the Brenners teach different courses in their own specialties, have separate offices and keep different hours. "Our fields overlap only to a degree," says Pat, who teaches statistics and international economics, while Steve lectures in U.S. economic history. Though they split one salary, they're both earning credit toward tenure. Because of the arrangement, Steve has more time to work on his Ph.D. thesis and Pat has the assurance that she won't be forced to quit when they have children.

The Brenners' happy accommodation is matched by Grinnell's satisfaction with the plan. "It gives us an opportunity to get more women on the faculty," says Dean Waldo S. Walker. "And we get more for our money. Two people expend 125% on the job and add an extra degree of expertise in small departments."

Mindful of these advantages, colleges across the country are giving job-sharing a whirl. Stanford University, Massachusetts Institute of Technology, Hamline University and colleges like Carleton, Oberlin, Hampshire and Gustavus Adolphus all have at least one couple sharing a single faculty position and say they want more. Dozens of other schools, including Colorado College, Bucknell University and the University of Delaware, say they are considering the concept.

"It will be universal in time," says Felice Schwartz, president of Catalyst Inc., a New York women's organization that explores nontraditional work patterns. "Our whole society is moving toward part-time work, as women want to work and make a contribution, and men become less concerned with the Protestant ethic of work for work's sake."

Job-splitting isn't brand new, nor is it confined exclusively to college campuses. The Framingham, Mass., school system pioneered the idea in 1965, hiring elementary-school teachers in pairs. In 1968, the Massachusetts welfare department hired 50 half-time women for 25 full-time social-worker slots. More recently, the Federal Reserve Bank in Boston allowed two people to split an assistant vice president post.

Job-splitting comes naturally to some couples with similar credentials. The careers of Adam and Maureen Yagodka, for example, have run parallel almost from the start. Both hold Ph.D.s in human ecology from the University of Oklahoma and worked together training a Job Corps staff and as consultants to Oklahoma's health department before taking a joint position at M.I.T. There, they work as a team, designing and implementing programs for the school's nonacademic employes.

"Because we're both interested in the same thing, we've taken a definite stand on working together as equals," says Maureen. The couple turned down one joint offer to do consulting work after their supervisor introduced only Adam at a conference and indicated salary and benefits would be in his name. "It sounded more and more like Maureen would be coming along as a volunteer," says Adam.

Not all joint positions call for identical credentials. For nearly two years, Linda Gillies and Cynthia Lambros shared a job setting up exhibits at the Metropolitan Museum of Art in New York. The two friends had worked together previously and suggested the plan to museum officials when they were both looking for parttime work. Because Mrs. Gillies had more experience and an edge in academic credentials, she was made assistant curator at an annual half-time salary of $7,000. Mrs. Lambros worked as a research assistant for $6,000 a year. "It gave me an opportunity to learn a whole new area," Mrs. Lambros says.

Although job-sharing may seem more suited to the university environment than the more rigid work schedules of private industry, some experts predict it will eventually be commonplace in the business world as well. "There's no question that job-splitting (in industry) will happen in the reasonably near future," says David Meredith, a specialist in manpower planning at McKinsey Co. in New York. As companies find it increasingly difficult to get qualified people who are willing to work full time, he says, "management will begin questioning whether it needs one person for eight specific hours."

The big push to hire more women may speed the introduction of job-sharing in business, just as it has on campus. College administrators, under stiff pressure to meet federal affirmative action requirements or risk losing precious federal funds, have seized on job-sharing as a way of recruiting more female faculty members. Small, rural colleges are leading the way because they have the most difficulty recruiting women. For example, Oberlin College in Oberlin, Ohio, offered a young couple a joint post in its psychology department. Norman Henderson, department chairman, explains: "A small, Midwestern town like ours isn't a place an unmarried woman would be happy with. Couples are more likely to settle here."

The Oberlin couple has also added welcome diversity to the small department. "We've got a dual person," says Mr. Henderson. "She's more interested in language development, he in cognitive thinking." Moreover, he says, the wife taught a course in the psychology of women that the school wouldn't otherwise have been able to offer.

Much of the pressure to create shared teaching positions still comes from the couples themselves. Largely because of an extremely tight academic job market, colleges report a deluge of applications from younger couples seeking to begin mutual careers. (One pair of Carleton hopefuls billed themselves as the "dynamic duo.") For older couples, job-sharing gives established professors more time for research while allowing their wives to resume teaching careers.

In 1971, for example, Pat Dean suggested at a faculty party that she share husband William's $15,000 tenured position in the religion department at Gustavus Adolphus College, St. Peter, Minn. Mrs. Dean, who had interrupted her own teaching career to have children, was startled when the dean dared her to have a proposal ready for the following Monday. Now she is teaching women's studies at the college, and she and her husband share housework and child-care duties. William is pleased with the arrangement because it allows him far more time for research.

College administrators agree that couple teams work much harder than one full-time teacher. Oberlin, in fact, is so afraid of exploiting its teaching couple that it bars them from campus one day a week.

Job-splitting couples cost colleges a little more in dual travel expenses and larger Social Security payments on two salaries. And the arrangement complicates the disbursement of certain employe benefits, such as retirement insurance and disability payments.

But colleges are far more concerned about the complications that could arise if a couple divorces. To minimize the impact of a divorce, schools usually place job-splitting couples in the same department and write separate part-time contracts specifying the exact amount of time each partner will put in. Some colleges specify that if one partner leaves, the other must fill the vacancy by working full-time.

Another potential trouble spot is the matter of tenure. Most colleges allow regular part-time staff to accumulate tenure credit, some at the same rate as full-time teachers, others in double the number of years. But this practice is by no means universal; Gustavus Adolphus refuses tenure credit to part-timers working less than half time, thus excluding three of the four wives currently sharing jobs with their husbands.

All colleges insist on making separate tenure decisions about each partner, and this is worrisome to many couple teams. "Can you imagine the horrendous complaints by the injured party if one gets it and the other doesn't?" says Margaret Rumbarger, associate secretary of the American Association of University Professors. To guard against such disappointments, colleges choose only highly qualified people for job-sharing arrangements. "We don't consider a couple if one is strong and the other isn't," says Oberlin's Mr. Henderson. "They each have to be even better than one full-timer."

1974   —LIZ ROMAN GALLESE

Changing Images—and Lives

"IN the beginning, women were usually pregnant, so the men hunted and fished while the women stayed home."

So begins the tale of women's oppression as told by Cranky Productions, a theater group appearing on and around the San Diego State College campus. Accompanied by the sounds of drums, tambourine and oboe, the narrator uses drawings to trace the second-class status of women from caveman days to modern times. One drawing shows a sad-faced woman with the word "inferior" stamped on her forehead.

To improve the self-image of women and alleviate injustices, the production suggests that the women in the audience enroll in the college's women's studies program, which sponsors Cranky. Courses in the program, founded in 1970, discuss such subjects as the role of women in history and literature and how society allegedly encourages feminine docility. The object is to help women understand their "oppression," so that they can do something about it.

Like black studies courses a few years ago, women's studies programs now are proliferating. In 1971, American colleges and universities offered at least 200 courses in women's studies, up from only 17 the year before, estimates Know Inc., a Pittsburgh publisher of feminist literature. More than 100 colleges now offer such courses.

154

At some campuses, the courses are having a drastic impact and creating a lively controversy. Many courses encourage militant feminism, and the programs have even prompted a few students to divorce their husbands.

In a variety of ways, the courses help students understand the status of women. At the start of a Cornell University women's history course, students were asked to list 12 famous American women who lived before 1900. "Nobody could do it," says senior Deborah Spitz, a teaching assistant in the course. "Now I expect all of them could."

At San Diego State, a course in human sexuality attempts to improve women's concept of themselves. A recent meeting of the course started with a seemingly innocuous film called "Why Man Creates." This depicted men working diligently in laboratories, doing research and studying. Women were shown as mothers, helpers to the men and ornaments. "This is what I call an obscene film," Prof. Lois Kessler told the class. Contending the film conveyed a "sexist" view of men creating while women merely watched, she asked the class, "What kind of image does woman have after seeing films like this her whole life?"

The most commonly taught courses deal with women in literature, as either authors or characters. At Mount Holyoke College in Massachusetts, Prof. James Ellis says he offered a course in 1970 called "Daughters and Ducats," which he said examined "the near-chattel status of women in matchmaking arrangements and the vicious double-standard accompanying this most prominently in Restoration Comedy." (A ducat is a gold coin.)

Some courses are changing lives. At Douglass College, the women's branch of New Jersey's Rutgers University, Prof. Elaine Showalter says students have actually gotten divorced after taking her women's studies course. "Although their husbands threaten me, I can't feel it was my fault," she says. The coursework led to "a process of sensitizing women to the political and cultural aspects of their lives. . . . They now find that motivation can work in fields besides housework," she says.

At the same college, a girl was planning to take a job and pay her fiance's way through medical school. After taking a women's studies course, she decided she wanted to attend medical school, too. Result: she and her fiance agreed they would both attend. The boy will go first—but only because he's older, the girl insists.

At the University of Washington, women's studies led one instructor to revert to use of her maiden name and later to divorce her husband. She has since turned her home into a halfway house where women in the midst of divorce proceedings live together and adjust to their changed way of life.

The courses often lead to political activity too. At San Diego State, students in the program sell feminist literature, give speeches to the community and support legislators working on pro-feminist bills. They picketed a bridal product exhibition that they contended treated women as a consumer but not as a person. "Why does he make the decision and she make dinner?" one picket sign asked.

Picketing and other outside activites aren't part of the regular course work. Such activities are voluntary, but they are encouraged in class, and many women do choose to volunteer.

Students praise the activism of the programs. The women's studies program "is an instrument of the larger feminist movement," says San Diego State student Pam Cole. "Ultimately it's an organizing tool, getting a woman to realize her own oppression so she can deal with it."

The activist aspects of the new courses worry some faculty members, however. Some feel the courses mainly reiterate women's liberation cliches. Women activists in such programs "all talk as if they ordered their words from Sears-Roebuck," complains James Julian, a journalism professor at the college.

But such reservations aren't stopping women's studies. In fact, the courses are even appealing to men. Of the 500 Cornell students enrolled in women's studies courses this year, 100 were male. At San Diego State, men can't vote at the program's meetings, but still constitute 10% of the enrollment. Bill Ritter, a student in the college's women in history course, feels such study "will eliminate any male chauvinism I have left in me."

Even in some high schools, women's studies are on the way. Sydney Spiegel, social studies teacher at East High School in Cheyenne, Wyo., says he will teach an elective course next year on the history of women. Mr. Spiegel, who taught a black history course earlier, says the course is already attracting a great deal of attention.

1971   —Barbara Isenberg

Mrs. Suzy Coed

CAROLYN G. Cohen found herself with little to do after her three children grew up. So, after a lapse of 32 years, she returned to college, majored in sociology at the University of Missouri and earned a bachelor's degree. And Mrs. Cohen, now 54 years old, enjoyed that so much she has gone on to graduate school.

"It has given me an aim," she says. "I used to think there was nothing for someone my age. Now I'd like to become a guidance counselor in a high school or junior college."

Mrs. Cohen is one of a legion of older women who have started or gone back to college in recent years. No exact figures are kept, but college officials estimated there were close to 500,000 women over 30 on the nation's campuses in the fall of 1972, about double the attendance of a decade prior to that.

Between 1960 and 1972, the number of women over 30 at the University of Washington rose to 1,923 from 759—a growth rate twice that of the student body as a whole. The University of North Carolina at Greensboro registered 179 women undergraduates over 28 years old in 1971, a 59% increase in four years. In 1972, the University of Wisconsin had 1,343 women at least 28 years old; in 1964 there were only 924 aged 25 and up.

The reasons for this movement are varied. Increased affluence has meant that more women have the money to pursue a costly college career. Labor-saving devices for the home and so-called convenience foods have given them more leisure time.

Changing ideas about the role of the American woman also have played a part. Not long ago, a woman who suddenly returned to college or embarked on a career after age 30 was viewed as unusual. If she had children at home, she ran the risk of being accused of neglecting them. But today, as the women's liberation movement grows, a middle-class woman who *doesn't* have an educational or career goal is likely to be looked down upon in some communities. "The home is no place to stay," contends Esther Westervelt, an educational consultant and former college administrator. "It has no real economic function, and society doesn't respect anything that doesn't have an economic function."

Some women even find that further education improves home life. "A lot of marriages get stale, and you have to put something new into them," says Eleanor Driver, director of the Continuous Center for Women at Oakland University in Oakland, Mich. "We're discovering that the task of the middle years is to save marriages." Recognizing that husbands with advanced degrees often "outgrow" their spouses, Purdue University offers grants to the wives of its graduate students, enabling them to take one or two courses a year. Since 1968, more than $20,000 has gone to 273 wives.

Colleges like having these older students around. For one thing, says Myrtle S. Jacobson, associate dean at Brooklyn College, "they're a little less rambunctious" than younger students. Frequently, they're also a source of sorely needed money at little additional expense; extra chairs usually can be squeezed into existing classes, and meals or dormitory space aren't required. Thus, to encourage women to return, colleges are offering a variety of special programs, counseling and job-placement services.

Most "mature" women are unable to obtain financial aid because they aren't full-time students, but some schools are beginning to offer scholarships. The University of Michigan has awarded $18,000 in fellowships to 20 women between 21 and 43 who had been out of school from one to 22 years. Part-time students were included.

"There's no reason these women shouldn't have the same benefits as anyone else," says Jean W. Campbell, director of the university's Center for Continuing Education for Women. Another program for part-timers, financed from a trust fund administered by Radcliffe College, has distributed fellowships from $300 to $2,500 to women graduate students at a number of Massachusetts, Connecticut and Rhode Island schools.

Returning to the books often proves difficult. Barbara Dennis, a housewife with two children in Evanston, Ill., quit her part-time speech and theater studies just a few courses short of a degree. Commuting five days a week to the University of Illinois campus in downtown Chicago took too long, she says, and her theater work sometimes kept her there until 2 a.m. "It was hard to compete with younger people who had more time," she says. "I felt burned out."

Some colleges realize this and try to make the grind easier. Marymount College at Loyola University, a women's school of 800 in Los Angeles, gives its older coeds the same courses as its young undergraduates but in separate classrooms. In that way, returning women don't have to worry about keeping up with the teen-age competition. Marymount also charges its older students only $75 a course instead of the standard $205.

Brooklyn College, a New York commuter school, has a "Small College" division for adults that meets two evenings a week. It takes five years, instead of four, to earn a degree, but it has proved extremely popular. The program began with 38 students in 1968. In 1972 it had 500 students, nearly 70% of whom are women. "We wanted something that adults could call their own and not feel lost in," says Myrtle Jacobson, associate dean.

Brooklyn also offers a special baccalaureate-degree program that awards up to half the credits necessary for graduation on the basis of an adult's previous job and experience. For example, a student who had lived with an Indian tribe received credit for several anthropology courses. A dancer was given credit for physical education.

Spalding College, a liberal-arts school in Louisville, rescheduled its three-day-a-week courses for slightly longer sessions two days a week, making it easier for housewives. The school also has a day-care center where a mother can leave a child for $1.50 a day.

Some women, like those in Tucson, attend lectures without venturing out of their living rooms. The University of Arizona offers several courses, including chemistry and horticulture, over its own television station. Students come to campus once a month or so to discuss their programs with a graduate student assistant.

In October 1971, the State University of New York system created Empire College, a network of one-building campuses across the state where adults study at their own pace. About half of the 400 students are women, mainly in their late 20s. With credit for previous job experience, a few students had to work only six months for their degrees. Study is for the most part independent, and students are graded on a pass-fail basis.

Where grades are given, college officials say their returning women do very well, often better than their teen-age counterparts. For example, 81% of the women in George Washington University's off-campus program in 1971 at 22 suburban Maryland and Virginia sites earned either As or Bs.

"A woman coming back at this stage of her life is going to be pretty serious about the whole thing," says Cecilia Zissis, director of Purdue's "Span" program for older women. Brooklyn's Dean Jacobson observes: "If you tell a young freshman to read 20 books, she'll read five or six and coast. Our returning women will read them all."

In addition, noncredit courses are proliferating for women who have finished raising families and are at a loss what to do next. In 1972, Salem College, a woman's school in Winston-Salem, N.C., opened an education and job-counseling center where for $50 a woman may attend 12 weekly sessions to help her "explore her identity, self-awareness and individual potential."

One woman who attended a similar program at the nearby Greensboro campus of the University of North Carolina is Janis Newton. "I had three children and was a corporation wife in a small textile town, going to tea parties and being a lady bountiful," Mrs. Newton recalls. "I knew that was a dead end."

A 1955 graduate of the Rhode Island School of Design, Mrs. Newton decided in 1967 to try for a master's degree in painting at the University of North Carolina. She soon discovered, however, that she had "changed, become more service oriented" and signed up for a self-awareness seminar. In 1970, Mrs. Newton, by then divorced, was leading a special seminar to help newly divorced women with their problems. Since then she has become an assistant director of continuing education in public health at the university. "I'm leading a fuller life now," she says.

Even with the multitude of special programs, some college administrators feel they aren't reaching everyone they should. "Most everything available is aimed at white, middle-class ladies," one official says. "We haven't been able to attract the disadvantaged element to any extent at all, probably because the education establishment is a symbol of failure and source of embarrassment to them."

Some schools are trying to change that. Since 1970, Jackson College for Women, a part of Tufts University, has "focused on low-income, inner-city blacks in the Boston area," says Judith Laskaris, associate dean. The program can offer only five scholarships of $3,050 a year, however, says Miss Laskaris, and most women have to work to get through."

Syracuse University "deliberately attempts to recruit high-risk students—those not normally admissible but who we think have potential," says Dean Alex Charters. The students, mainly inner-city blacks and about half of them women, get college credit for preparatory reading courses and are expected to move on to the regular college curriculum afterwards. The students don't pay any fees; the cost is divided between the university and the state of New York.

1972   —DAVID M. ELSNER

Sexism and Schools

WHEN Theresa Hickey of Homerville, Ohio, prepared to enter seventh grade in the fall of 1973, she ran into a problem. The folks at Black River Junior High School wouldn't let her enroll.

At least they wouldn't let her enroll in industrial arts, a class involving the use of tools, woodworking and so on. Instead, officials of the school informed her that because she was a girl, she was required to study home economics.

"That just made me sick," says Theresa, a well-mannered 12-year-old who lives on a farm in this rural community about 50 miles southwest of Cleveland. "What I really wanted to learn about was how to use tools, a hammer and saw, things like that. After all, I've been learning how to cook and keep house since I was in a high chair."

Theresa's father, a lawyer who practices in Cleveland, wrote to the school board asking that Theresa be permitted to take industrial arts. He got a flat rejection. When all else failed, Theresa sought help from Women's Law Fund Inc., a year-old nonprofit group in Cleveland active in women's rights. Acting on Theresa's behalf, the group sued in federal district court, and the school board quickly reversed its policy.

Larry E. Rodenberger, superintendent of the Black River School District, and a defendant in Theresa's suit, says, "The sex equality thing is having a big impact in the schools, particularly as far as staffing and physical facilities are concerned. We're having to rethink just about everything we've traditionally done. The problem is gigantic."

Indeed, sex discrimination in public education is coming under attack in school systems across the country. Groups of feminists, parents, teachers and youngsters themselves are pressing for change on a variety of fronts. The issues range from classes that exclude one or the other sex to casual remarks made by teachers to athletic program funding and to the fairness of materials used in the classrooms.

Almost no one denies that a problem exists. "Like it or not, in the past the educational system has tended to point girls to certain types of careers and boys toward others," says John C. Pittenger, Pennsylvania's Secretary of Education who in 1972 ordered school officials to end all discriminatory activities. "On balance, I think it's accurate to say that education hasn't been fair to anybody—not to boys or girls, their mothers and fathers, or to teachers and administrators."

Fairness is what the fuss is all about. Much of the controversy involves texts and other teaching materials. In a number of locations, parents, teachers and others are objecting because they feel teaching materials are unfairly biased to show the actions and achievements of boys.

"The over-riding message is that boys, not blondes, have more fun," says Jo Jacobs, the mother of three children in Kalamazoo, Mich., who is heading a crusade aimed at bringing elementary reading texts published by Houghton Mifflin Co. into "balance." "Reading the books," she adds, "you can't help but get the feeling that a boy is the better thing to be."

Among other things, Mrs. Jacobs and other members of the Committee to Study Sex Discrimination in the Kalamazoo Public Schools complained that the books showed only 40 occupations for women, compared with 215 for men. "Throughout the books, the major female character is mother," Mrs. Jacobs says. "She's always available, always at home, always cooking or mending, always ready to kiss and make things better. They totally ignored the fact that half of the mothers with children aged 6 to 17 work."

Mrs. Jacobs' group was formed to advise the school system on sex discrimination matters. It filed an administrative complaint in 1973 with the Department of Health, Education and Welfare, alleging violations of a federal law prohibiting sex discrimination in schools receiving federal funds. The complaint came when the Kalamazoo schools bought the Houghton Mifflin books for use during that year.

After filing its complaint, and with the cooperation of the local school system, the group labored throughout the summer annotating and rewriting major portions of the texts and teachers' manuals to make more mention of girls, their activities and their accomplishments. The reworked texts—cut up and with supplemental material pasted in—are currently in use in the Kalamazoo schools.

"We could have told this committee, this group of parents, to go to hell, but we didn't," says Morris J. Hamilton, director of elementary education in Kalamazoo. "We chose, instead, to work with them."

Neither the Kalamazoo schools nor Mrs. Jacobs' group places much blame on Houghton Mifflin because they agree that the texts involved are among the best on the market. The problem, they say, is that almost all texts contain sex bias. John T. Ridley, a Houghton Mifflin editor, says one of the problems for publishing concerns and other suppliers is that not enough unbiased material is available for use in books. Mr. Ridley adds that many of the changes written into the texts in Kalamazoo "will be incorporated into future editions."

A major reason behind such changes is an upsurge of interest on the part of parents and educators in sex discrimination and its possible effects on the aspirations, ambitions and mental outlooks of children. In fact, school officials in almost every part of the country concede that they're under growing pressure, particularly from parents.

Typical of the groups springing up is one in Seattle that calls itself "Citizens for Elimination of Sex Role Stereotyping in Public Education." According to Sally Mackle, the mother of two preschoolers and a substitute high-school teacher, the group got going early in 1973 when another mother and a community organizer "got to discussing the subject."

David Wagoner, a lawyer in Seattle who's president of the Board of Education, recalls his first contact with the group. "First off, they wrote us a letter expressing a number of concerns about sex discrimination," he says. "We invited them to meet with us, and they showed us slides of books we were using in the school system. They went into the idea that the books showed men in all the interesting jobs in business and the professions, while women were shown mainly in the home." As a result of the complaints, a major study of sex role stereotyping in the Seattle schools has been launched. "We're looking at everything—from teacher attitudes to textbooks —from kindergarten through grade 12," says Dave Kroft, director of staff development for the Seattle schools.

In Seattle and a number of other locations, teacher attitude is a serious concern. "We've had tremendous sexism. It was widespread and commonly practiced," says Andrades Smith, coordinator of counseling services at Community High School in Ann Arbor, Mich. "It went all the way from the hiring of teachers and administrators to career counseling of students and everyday things in the classrooms." Partly as a result of pressure brought by militant feminists both inside and outside the school system, training seminars for teachers were organized to explore subtle and overt sex discrimination at Community High. In addition to talks by a female lawyer and other professionals, the seminars featured a lesson in role reversal: Male teachers served the coffee. Similar seminars are planned for all teachers in the Ann Arbor school system, during the current school year.

On a related front, athletic programs are under attack in several spots. In Waco, Texas, for instance, the Women's Equity Action League, a women's rights group, filed a complaint in 1973 alleging sex discrimination in athletics and other areas. The complaint, which is stiffly disputed by officials in the school system, contends that $250,000 is allotted annually to a variety of boys' athletic programs, while girls are permitted to play only tennis, with an allotment of $970.

Several other aspects of educational funding, particularly at the high school and college levels, appear certain to be challenged. Women's Law Fund, the Cleveland group, plans to file a federal lawsuit against a Big 10 university, alleging sex discrimination in the allocation of financial aid. Rita Reuss, chief counsel at the Women's Law Fund, declines to identify the university involved. She contends, "It looks like it's all tied to the jock psychology—the idea that men are the only ones who do things, who have to earn a living. So they're the ones who get most of the scholarship money."

Perhaps the most persuasive element in the drive to end sex discrimination in the schools is action on their own behalf by youngsters, such as Theresa Hickey, the

Ohio farm girl who took her case to court. Sharon Bod-ensteiner, a history teacher in Seattle's Cleveland High School, tells of the time when three girl students approached her to express their concern about sex discrimination. One result was the establishment of a six-week "mini-course" in feminism.

Jean King, a lawyer in Ann Arbor, says her 14-year-old daughter, Nancy, "came home from school really worked up about sexist remarks in the classroom." Mrs. King says that when one teacher, a man, asked for "two strong-armed boys" to volunteer to carry books, Nancy stood up at once and declared the request to be sexist.

"It implied that girls weren't capable of carrying books," Mrs. King says. Two other girls promptly sided with Nancy and volunteered for the chores. Taking on teachers on a head-to-head basis can be risky, of course, but Mrs. King adds that "the kids are very smart about this kind of thing." Nancy, she says, "chose her target well—she was careful to pick a fairly young and with-it guy." Two girls ended up carrying the books.

1973   —EVERETT GROSECLOSE

Graham, ET

WHAT DO WOI

Chicopee, I

169 pages

WO